Stadium Stories:

Tennessee Volunteers

Colorful Tales of the Orange and White

Randy Moore

Stadium Stories is a trademark of Morris Book Publishing, LLC.

Text design: Casey Shain
All photos are courtesy of the University of Tennessee Sports Information Department.
The publisher gratefully acknowledges Ruby Goodman for permission to print the lyrics to "Go Holloway," written by her late husband, Ted Goodman.

Library of Congress Cataloging-in-Publication Data
Moore, Randy, 1952–
    Stadium Stories : Tennessee Volunteers / Randy Moore.
        p. cm. – (Stadium stories series)
    ISBN 0-7627-3140-0
      1. Tennessee Volunteers (Football team) 2. University of Tennessee–Football–History.
    I. Title: Tennessee Volunteers. II. Title. III. Series.

GV958.U586M66 2004
796.332'63'0976885--dc22   2004051808

Manufactured in the United States of America
First Edition/First Printing

For Cindy:
I wish you could have lived to see this day.

Contents

Big Orange Football

U niversity of Tennessee football is more than a Saturday afternoon diversion. It is a happening that begins on fall Mondays and steadily gains momentum until kickoff, by which time the pulse-pounding tension is almost unbearable.

It is 107,000 fans squeezing into Neyland Stadium and hundreds of thousands more gathering around TVs and radios—cheering every completion, celebrating every touchdown, hanging on every word.

It is the 200 boats that make up the "Volunteer Navy" cruising along the Tennessee River, then docking across the street from the stadium for the nautical equivalent of tailgating.

It is orange-and-white checkerboard end zones, General Neyland's game maxims, and public address announcer Bobby Denton eliciting cheers by noting a tackle made by "a host of Volunteers."

It is great players such as Beattie Feathers, George Cafego, Bob Suffridge, Hank Lauricella, Doug Atkins, Johnny Majors, Condredge Holloway, Reggie White, and Peyton Manning.

It is such unforgettable plays as Johnny Butler's serpentine run, "The Stop" on Billy Cannon, and Holloway's electrifying two-point conversion pass to Larry Seivers.

It is a four-quarter melodrama played out each week on a freshly mowed stage before the world's most animated audience.

It is a draining yet exhilarating roller-coaster ride that always leaves its customers clamoring for more.

In short, Big Orange football has a flavor all its own. The eleven stories contained within these pages represent a determined attempt to capture that flavor.

Military Precision

Robert R. Neyland had such an uncanny knack for seeing every block and tackle made during his University of Tennessee football practices that some players suspected he had eyes in the back of his head.

He didn't, of course. In fact, he didn't need the ones in the *front* of his head. He proved as much on November 30, 1938.

Three days before the Volunteers were to close the regular season against the University of Mississippi, Major Neyland—he would not achieve the rank of general until many years later—gathered his troops to stage a little amateur magic show. Draping a towel over his face to create the effect of a blindfold, he ordered his first-team offensive players to line up in their trademark single-wing formation. He went on to explain that the deep snap, as always, would go to tailback George Cafego, who would then hand the ball to the blindfolded coach.

"I'll show you just how simple this is," Neyland vowed.

And that's precisely what he did. On cue, the ball was snapped to Cafego, who quickly handed the pigskin to the coach. Neyland retreated a step, paused briefly, then unleashed a pass that sliced through the nippy November air, finding its way into the outstretched arms of the left end just as he made his cut toward the middle of the field.

The players were amazed; The Major was amused—so amused that he repeated the trick. This time a halfback ran 10 yards downfield, pivoting just as Neyland's blind but deadly accurate pass hit him squarely in the stomach.

The Volunteers had seen enough to be dumbfounded, but The Major was just getting started. Four more times he took the handoff from Cafego and threw blindly toward a Tennessee receiver. One pass wobbled and fell short of its intended target, but the other three were right on the mark. Having sufficiently dazzled his audience, Neyland removed the towel from his face and deadpanned, "That's all."

None of the Volunteers were surprised by The Major's arm strength. After all, he had been a standout pitcher in his baseball days. What shocked them was the precision—military precision, perhaps—with which he delivered pass after pass to an unseen moving target.

Through one dramatic display, Neyland underscored the value of timing in offensive football. By counting in unison under their breath for a predetermined number of seconds, the passer and receiver could operate with the efficiency of a fine Swiss timepiece. The message was delivered; the lesson was learned. Three days later, a finely tuned Tennessee squad battered Mississippi 47–0 to conclude a 10–0 regular season.

The power running game was Neyland's passion, but he proved to be an astute pupil of the passing game as well. The so-called "timing route" he displayed on that fateful day in 1938 would become a staple of offensive football, along with many more of his teachings.

Although Neyland's blindfolded pass was a clever parlor trick that effectively relaxed his players before a big game, his knowledge and utilization of psychology went much further. He was a master of mind games as well as football games.

Playing in a driving rainstorm at Birmingham in 1932, his Volunteers trailed Alabama 3–0 at halftime. All the armchair quarterbacks in the stands assumed that The Major would

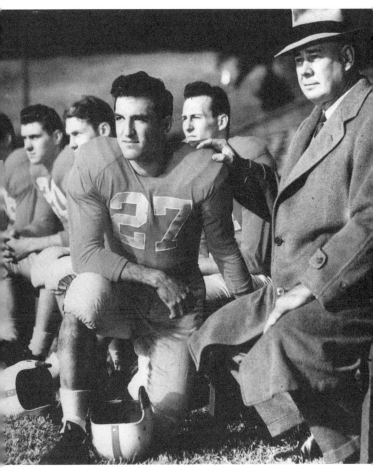

Robert R. Neyland, pictured with Hank Lauricella (27), had his coaching career interrupted twice by military responsibilities. As a result, he served three stints as Tennessee's head man—1926–34, 1936–40, and 1946–52.

elect to play the third quarter with the wind at his team's back—but he was two steps ahead of them.

"We'll give Alabama the wind in the third quarter," Neyland told his troops. "They have a lead to protect, and they'll have to be conservative, taking no chances on a sloppy field. We'll get the wind in the fourth quarter; we'll be able to strike, and they will be helpless to stop us or retaliate."

Sure enough, the Crimson Tide played cautiously throughout the third quarter, content to protect its 3–0 lead. Taking full advantage of the wind in the final period, Tennessee gained ground on each exchange of punts and eventually scored the go-ahead touchdown on a run by Beattie Feathers to prevail 7–3.

In addition to being a brilliant student of human nature, Neyland was a strict disciplinarian who drilled his players much as West Point instructors had drilled him years earlier. He gradually instilled his innate toughness—mental and physical—into the willing Volunteers. They played hurt. They played tired. They played hard. They played together. They played well.

Two of the greatest compliments ever accorded Tennessee's legendary head man came from peers. Disdaining the argument that great players make great coaches, Alabama's Wallace Wade said of Neyland: "He could take his and beat yours, or he could take yours and beat his."

After a 21–0 defeat of Alabama in 1939 extended Neyland's string of consecutive victories to seventeen, he received lavish praise from Jock Sutherland, who had won a national championship at Pittsburgh just two years earlier. Noting that the Volunteers "would beat any team in the country, and that goes for the pro teams," Sutherland added: "Major Neyland's (work) at Tennessee exceeds anything I've ever seen in all my football experience. There were no flaws in the Tennessee team."

That, of course, was by design. Neyland didn't demand perfection, but he clearly expected it. The first of his famous game maxims held that "the team that makes the fewest mistakes will win." Toward this end he emphasized simplicity, limiting his Tennessee teams to two dozen offensive plays and four basic defenses. To further reduce the risk of mistakes, he insisted: "No offensive play should be used in a game until it has been rehearsed 500 times."

Whereas coaching contemporary Knute Rockne of Notre Dame gained fame for his emotionally charged pregame speeches—"Win one for the Gipper" being the most memorable—Neyland carefully avoided motivational histrionics.

"Resolution and determination; that's what's going to win today" was as close as he came to a fiery pep talk. Sometimes, if he was in an especially glib mood, Neyland would point out that the opponent could not beat Tennessee because "they do not have the background." Otherwise the Volunteers' head man left the rhetoric to others.

"Pregame harangues, as a rule, do more harm than good," he once said. "Inspiration at zero hour is a poor thing to rely on."

Neyland stated this belief in even more graphic language while instructing his team prior to a 1928 game against the University of Florida. "Some teams dash out on the field with tears in their eyes to do or die for alma mater," he said. "If you go out there with tears in your eyes, you won't be able to see the ball. I want you to see it."

The dry-eyed Volunteers won 13–12.

Instead of melodramatic pep talks, Neyland relied on intense preparation and well-planned strategy. He waged a football game much as a military leader wages a battle—calmly,

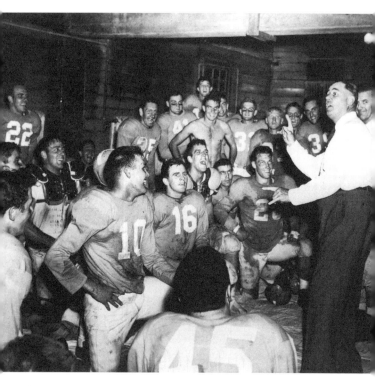

Although he was a no-nonsense disciplinarian, Neyland often led his players in song following a big victory.

forcefully, strategically—careful to remain detached from the furor surrounding him while determining how to maximize the efficiency of his troops. He composed lengthy lists of football principles, which he adhered to religiously, and kept voluminous notes, which he revisited regularly, including:

- Never lose the ball on downs.
- Speed up the play in scoring zone and when we have the wind.

- In wet weather with a muddy field, it is best to kick a lot and let opponents do the fumbling.
- The head coach must remain a little aloof from the players and, to a certain extent, from the coaches.
- Football is composed of nothing but accidents: The great art is to profit from such accidents. This is the mark of genius.
- Nature of the struggle between equal teams. The difference: never physical but invariably mental.
- To defeat a weak opponent is not the problem: The problem is to win when he is as good or better than you.
- Almost all close games are lost by the losers . . . not won by the winners.

Neyland was widely perceived as an ultraconservative, and understandably so. He began a four-item list of Offensive Principles with "Conservative in the main. Gamble when necessary," and ended with "Avoid game-losing errors." His so-called Defensive Outline included such gems as "There are more ways to score on defense than on offense," and "We will trade possession for position whenever it's to our advantage."

Still, the man was not averse to the occasional risk. His notes underscore this point, as well.

For instance:

- Take a chance. When behind, open up with tricks and passes, etc. You have nothing to lose and everything to gain. If convinced the game is an even break, gamble near the end of the halves.
- If you have a man who can pass a wet ball, passes are very effective on wet days.
- If this pass be used in an obvious plunge (running) situation, say third down and one to gain, the inherent surprise

value of the play is enormously increased.

- Don't save your passing game until you are behind; it won't work then.
- When six points or more behind, you want a touchdown. Gamble for it with a pass, fake pass, tricks, or other long gainers.
- Mix up your attack. . . . Don't get in the habit of using your downs in such a methodical manner that opponents are able to guess your plays.

Neyland's notes also reveal a keen opportunist who never overlooked a chance to exploit a situation. "If an opposing line man is groggy," he wrote, "shoot a play at him. If a back is limping, a forward pass into his territory should be productive of results."

Although he was a stickler for fair play, Neyland advocated intentionally violating the rules in order to preserve a lead in the closing minutes of a game. "In same situation, tackle dangerous pass receiver if necessary to prevent completion of the pass," he wrote. "The penalty can't beat you, but a completed pass might."

Finally, under the heading "Psychological plays early in the game," he wrote: "It is well to use special trick plays early in the game on opponents known to be high-strung and nervous."

Clearly complex and abundantly intriguing, Robert Reese Neyland was born February 17, 1892, in Greenville, Texas—the son of a lawyer (Robert) and a school teacher (Pauline). After establishing himself as a top-notch student in high school, he spent a year at Burleson Junior College and then studied engineering at Texas A&M. Earning an appointment to West Point, he gained fame through his brilliant athletic

Still the Master

Tennessee coaching legend Robert R. Neyland's brilliance as a teacher has been underscored by the remarkable success of his protégés. Dozens of his former players have gone on to become head coaches, including Hall of Famer Bowden Wyatt.

Another Neyland protégé was Bob Woodruff, who served as head man at the University of Florida in the 1950s. One day on the practice field, while puffing a cigar and chatting with Indiana coach and fellow Neyland product Phil Dickens, Woodruff noticed a visitor ambling toward them. Recognizing the guest as Neyland, Woodruff hastily discarded the cigar.

"What did you do that for?" Dickens asked. "He isn't your boss anymore."

"I know it," Woodruff replied, "but I'm not sure *he* does."

skills. He reigned for three years as the school's heavyweight boxing champ and established a 35–5 pitching record that included twenty consecutive victories. He was so highly regarded as a baseball prospect that he was offered contracts by several professional teams, including the Boston Red Sox, who already owned the rights to a young pitcher named George Herman "Babe" Ruth.

Choosing to pursue a military career, Neyland spurned big league baseball. After serving his country in World War I, he was hired by the University of Tennessee in 1925 as a Reserve Officer Training Corps (ROTC) instructor. For an additional $700 he would assist head football coach M. B. Banks. When Banks left a year later, Neyland was elevated to fill the void after just one season on staff. His charge from

Dean Nathan Dougherty was simple: "Do something about the series with Vanderbilt."

Neyland did. After losing to the powerful Commodores 20–3 in 1926, he forged a 7–7 tie in '27 and defeated them 6–0 in '28. He also prevailed in '29, '30, and '31; tied in '32; and then won in '33 and '34. He missed the 1935 season to serve in Panama but returned in 1936 to beat Vanderbilt four times over the next five years. After serving his country from 1941 to 1946 in World War II, Neyland—now a brigadier general—defeated the hated Commodores six times over his final seven seasons. His all-time record against Vanderbilt was a spectacular 16–3–2. The magnitude of that accomplishment can be truly appreciated only when viewed from the perspective that Tennessee's record against the Commodores prior to his arrival was 2–17–2.

Neyland's stature as the catalyst in Volunteer football history is beyond question. In 1925, the year before he assumed command, Tennessee's stadium held 3,200 fans and the program's net profit was $55.85. Within four years the stadium had swelled to 17,860 seats and the profits had made a similar quantum leap.

Although two stints in the Armed Services cost Neyland five years of his coaching prime, his feats still qualify as legendary. His first seven seasons produced sixty-one victories, two losses, and five ties. As a three-touchdown underdog, his 1928 team stunned Alabama 15–13 at Tuscaloosa in a game many observers believe launched Tennessee into elite status. He won thirty-three consecutive regular-season games between 1937 and 1941, including a remarkable seventeen shutouts in a row. His twenty-one-year coaching career shows 173 wins, 31 losses, and 12 ties, with a remarkable 112 shutouts. He put together nine undefeated regular seasons,

Game Maxims

Although Robert R. Neyland is credited with originating his famous "Game Maxims," he actually borrowed the idea from his college coach and then added some commandments of his own. Charles Dudley Daly, under whom Neyland played and coached at West Point, wrote a book called *American Football* that featured the following "Football Axioms":

- Football is a battle. Go out to fight and keep it up all the afternoon.
- A man's value to his team varies inversely as his distance from the ball.
- If the line goes forward the team wins; if the line comes backward the team loses.

Daly also listed three "Game Axioms" in his book:

- Make and play for the breaks. When one comes your way, score.
- If the game or a break goes against you, don't lie down—put on more steam.
- Don't save yourself. Go the limit. There are good men on the side line when you are exhausted.

Neyland eventually adapted these ideas to form his Game Maxims:

1. The team that makes the fewest mistakes will win.
2. Play for and make the breaks, and when one comes your way— SCORE.
3. If at first the game—or breaks—go against you, don't let up . . . put on more steam.
4. Protect our kickers, our QB, our lead, and our ball game.
5. Ball, oskie, cover, block, cut and slice, pursue and gang tackle . . . for this is the WINNING EDGE.
6. Press the kicking game. Here is where the breaks are made.
7. Carry the fight to our opponent, and keep it there for sixty minutes.

fielding a 1939 team that went unbeaten, untied, and unscored-upon. He claimed two Southern Conference titles, five Southeastern Conference championships, one consensus national title (1951), and three fractional national championships (1938, 1940, 1950). To this day his winning percentage of 82.9 is the finest of any head coach with at least twenty years experience.

In seven head-to-head meetings with Kentucky's Paul "Bear" Bryant, who would become a legend in his own right during a subsequent stint at Alabama, Neyland registered five victories and two ties. While attending Neyland's retirement banquet in 1953, Bryant grumbled, "Thank God the old guy finally quit."

Although not known as an innovator, Neyland is credited with being the first coach to use game films to evaluate his own team and scout opponents; outfit his backs and receivers in tearaway jerseys to help them break tackles; transmit information to the sidelines via a press box phone; and cover the field with a tarpaulin to limit water damage.

Based on his remarkable longevity and success, Neyland was elected to the College Football Hall of Fame in 1956. In a 1969 poll of the nation's top coaches, athletics directors, and sports writers, he finished second to Notre Dame's Rockne as "Football's Greatest Coach."

As happens with all longtime coaches, the General endured some rocky times. When Tennessee's record dipped to 5–5 in 1947 and 4–4–2 in 1948—the only nonwinning seasons in Neyland's career—fans with short memories began to criticize him. His open disdain for the two-platoon system— "rat race football," he called it—and his adamant refusal to scrap the antiquated single-wing in favor of the more fashionable T formation led some doubters to suggest the game had passed him by. A few detractors even called him a dinosaur. The grumbling became so loud and so widespread in 1949 that Peggy Neyland pleaded with her husband to step down. Naturally, he refused.

Two years later his 1951 team won Tennessee's first consensus national title.

The Streak

W hen Vanderbilt rallied from a 7–0 second-quarter deficit to defeat Tennessee 13–7 in Knoxville on November 13, 1937, none of the 3,000 fans in attendance could have foreseen what would follow. The Volunteers' head coach, Major Robert Neyland, hated losing to the Commodores, and this particular defeat must have been especially galling. It was to be the last regular-season game his Volunteers would lose for more than three years.

Tennessee won its next thirty-three consecutive regular-season outings, spanning the last two games of '37; all of '38, '39, and '40; plus the '41 opener. The only losses during this span occurred in bowl games—a 14–0 setback to Southern California in the 1940 Rose Bowl and a 19–13 loss to Boston College in the 1941 Sugar Bowl.

During this incredible thirty-three-game run, the Volunteers registered seventeen consecutive shutouts—an NCAA record that stands to this day. Ten of the shutouts occurred in 1939, when Tennessee was unbeaten, untied, and unscored-upon—the last major college program to accomplish this amazing feat.

What follows is a game-by-game recap of one of the most remarkable streaks in the history of athletic competition.

1937 Season

Tennessee 13, Kentucky 0: Playing in Lexington on Thanksgiving Day, November 26, 1937, Tennessee got back on track thanks to single-wing tailback George Cafego. His 71-yard rushing performance was so dazzling that when Cafego trotted back onto the field late in the game, Kentucky's radio announcer exclaimed, "Oh, no! Here comes that bad news again." Thus was born one of the great nicknames in school history, "Bad News" Cafego. After Cafego scored Tennessee's first touchdown on a 25-yard run in the second quarter, the Volunteers used some trickery to add an insurance touchdown in the third quarter. Backup tailback Babe Wood passed to Ralph Eldred, who lateralled the ball to Joe Little, who chugged across the goal line to complete the 16-yard scoring play.

Tennessee 32, Mississippi 0: Playing in Memphis, the Volunteers closed the 1937 season with a bang, exploding for twenty-five second-half points. The first half had been a defensive struggle, with the only score coming on a 45-yard interception return by Tennessee defensive back Melvin Herring, who then added the extra point. One-yard runs by Cafego, Marion Perkins, and Robert Sneed widened the gap to 26–0; and then Thomas "Red" Harp scored on a 6-yard lateral to complete the scoring.

1938 Season

Tennessee 26, Sewanee 3: The Volunteers struck for twenty first-quarter points, and then coasted in the 1938 opener, played September 24 in Knoxville. Bob Foxx started the rout with a 30-yard run on a reverse. Bowden Wyatt blocked a punt and recovered in the end zone for touchdown number two. Joe Wallen scored a third touchdown on a 16-yard "spinner," and Cheek Duncan added a fourth TD on a 4-yard double-reverse in the second quarter. Sewanee averted

Single-wing tailback George Cafego earned the colorful nickname "Bad News" with his stellar play against Kentucky in 1937.

a shutout by booting a 17-yard field goal in the fourth quarter.

Tennessee 20, Clemson 7: October 1 got off to a bad start as the Tigers stunned the homestanding Volunteers by scoring a second-quarter touchdown for a 7–0 lead. Moments later Tennessee pulled even, however, when Robert Andridge rambled 59 yards untouched on a reverse and Cafego kicked the point after touchdown. Fullback Leonard Coffman broke the tie with a 1-yard plunge in the third quarter, and Foxx returned an interception 23 yards for the clinching touchdown in the fourth.

Tennessee 7, Auburn 0: Wallen broke a scoreless tie in the fourth quarter by plowing into the end zone on third-and-goal at the Tiger 1 yard line. Wyatt kicked the extra point, and an unyielding Volunteer defense did the rest, as Tennessee moved to 3–0 with a dramatic victory.

Tennessee 13, Alabama 0: The Volunteers hadn't beaten the mighty Crimson Tide in six years when they ventured into Birmingham on October 15, but that was about to change. Coffman bulled over from inches away to give Tennessee a 6–0 first-quarter lead. Then, after Cafego rambled 33 yards in the third quarter, Coffman bulled into the end zone again—this time from a yard out. Wyatt kicked the point after touchdown (PAT), and Tennessee's reputation as a gridiron giant began to blossom. The Volunteers made their first appearance in the Associated Press national rankings a week later, checking in at number eight.

Tennessee 44, The Citadel 0: Foxx scored on runs of 7 and 12 yards to spark a twenty-seven-point second-quarter explosion that produced a 34–0 halftime bulge. Third-team tailback

Sneed showcased his passing skills by hitting Pryor Bacon with a 17-yard touchdown toss and later connecting with him on a conversion pass. Tennessee fine-tuned its kicking unit in the fourth quarter, scoring the game's last three points on a 20-yard field goal by Wyatt.

Tennessee 14, Louisiana State 6: A fourth-and-goal gamble paid dividends for Tennessee as Coffman plunged into the end zone from the 1-foot line for a first-quarter touchdown. Wyatt's PAT provided a 7–0 lead, but LSU scored on a 21-yard touchdown pass from Simes to Kavanaugh. The point-after failed, leaving Tennessee on top 7–6. Cafego widened the gap to 13–6 with a 2-yard touchdown burst in the third quarter, and Wyatt's PAT concluded the scoring.

Tennessee 45, Chattanooga 0: Elevated from number eight to number six in the Associated Press national rankings, the Volunteers proved worthy of the compliment by unleashing an unexpected weapon—the forward pass. Wyatt scored the game's first three touchdowns—grabbing a 41-yard pass from Buist Warren, plus tosses of 45 and 11 yards from Walter "Babe" Wood—as Tennessee rolled. Sneed completed a 12-yard touchdown pass to Bacon and later scored on a 12-yard burst up the middle. He also drop-kicked the PAT after each score.

Tennessee 14, Vanderbilt 0: Fourth-ranked Tennessee saw its nine-game winning streak in serious jeopardy as the Volunteers entered the final quarter of their November 12 game at Vanderbilt locked in a scoreless tie. Disdaining a short field-goal try, head coach Neyland ordered Wood to hit left tackle on fourth-and-goal at the Commodore 4 yard line. The play produced a touchdown, and Wyatt's conversion kick gave the

Bowden Wyatt captained the 1938 Volunteer team that got Tennessee's remarkable thirty-three-game regular-season streak rolling. He returned to his alma mater as head coach in 1955.

Volunteers a 7–0 lead. Later in the period Wyatt rambled 23 yards to the Vandy 4 yard line, from which point Wood scored again. Wyatt's PAT concluded the scoring and sealed Tennessee's tenth consecutive win.

Tennessee 46, Kentucky 0: After touchdown runs by Foxx (24 yards), Cafego (2 yards), Robert Andridge (12 yards), and Joe Wallen (3 yards) provided a 25–0 second-quarter lead, Tennessee turned to trickery for its next two scores. Sneed hit James Coleman with an 18-yard touchdown pass, and then Cheek Duncan scored on a 2-yard reverse as the lead swelled to 37–0. Tennessee added a safety early in the fourth quarter when, according to the official game summary, "UK center pass goes over end zone fence." Bacon tacked on a 27-yard touchdown run to secure the final margin.

Tennessee 47, Mississippi 0: Fullback Coffman, normally called on for short-yardage plunges, burst 52 yards to ignite a nineteen-point third-quarter eruption that carried the Volunteers to a smashing victory in the regular-season finale. Warren provided the day's most exciting play, returning a Rebel punt 86 yards for a score. Wyatt turned in a spectacular play as well, returning an interception 34 yards for another touchdown. Clearly picking up steam, the Volunteers had closed out the regular season by outscoring their final four opponents by a combined score of 152–0. Dunkel, Litkenhous, Board, Houlgate, and Poling tabbed Tennessee the national champ, but Associated Press voters relegated the Volunteers to the number-two spot behind Texas Christian in the final poll of 1938.

Note: Although it wasn't included in the thirty-three-game regular-season winning streak, Tennessee's appearance in the

Orange Bowl on New Year's Day of 1939 ranks with the most memorable outings in school history. Put bluntly, the Volunteers and fourth-ranked Oklahoma staged one of the dirtiest games in gridiron history. Major Neyland—he had not yet been promoted to his highest rank—was so upset by the tenor of the game that he sent even-tempered Joe Little into the lineup with instructions to "stop all the foolishness and play football." Alas, Little was banished from the game after one play . . . for fighting. Tennessee opened the scoring on an 8-yard reverse by Foxx and a 15-yard burst around right end by Wood. Wyatt booted a 22-yard field goal and scored another point when he scooped up his first conversion attempt (which was blocked) and raced into the end zone with the ball. Tennessee romped 17–0, concluding what many longtime fans consider the greatest season in school history.

1939 Season

Tennessee 13, North Carolina State 0: Newly elected captain Sam Bartholomew started the 1939 season in style on September 29 at Raleigh, returning the opening kickoff 79 yards to the North Carolina State 6 yard line. Foxx scored two plays later, on second-and-goal from the 4. Cafego found Andridge with a 9-yard scoring pass later in the quarter, booted the PAT, and then turned the game over to Tennessee's defense.

Tennessee 40, Sewanee 0: Neyland's methodical offensive system gave way to a big-play explosion on this day. Cafego scored on a 47-yard punt return and completed a 13-yard touchdown pass to Foxx, who also scored on an 11-yard run from scrimmage. Butler completed a 21-yard scoring pass to

William Barnes and added a 63-yard touchdown on a scrimmage run. Wallen joined the fun by scoring on a 38-yard burst up the middle.

Tennessee 28, Chattanooga 0: A nineteen-point second-quarter eruption settled Game 3 early, giving the visiting Volunteers a 25–0 halftime lead. Andridge scored on a 40-yard end run and a 19-yard pass from Warren. Fred Newman and Coffman had short touchdown runs, and Barnes closed the scoring with a 23-yard third-quarter field goal.

Tennessee 21, Alabama 0: Butler opened the scoring with a serpentine 56-yard touchdown run that some observers considered the greatest exhibition of rushing skill in program history. The Volunteers then salted away the victory with two fourth-quarter touchdowns—the first coming on an 11-yard scamper by Foxx, the second on a 13-yard burst by Warren off a fake reverse.

Tennessee 17, Mercer 0: Again showing a knack for the big play, the Volunteers struck for two first-period touchdowns. Butler got the initial touchdown on a 16-yard fourth-down run; Foxx got the second on a 70-yard ramble off right tackle. Newman tacked on a 25-yard field goal in the second quarter to conclude the scoring.

Tennessee 20, Louisiana State 0: One of the most revered strategies in football is to strike quickly following a turnover, and Tennessee did just that on this fateful day in Baton Rouge. The Volunteers' William Luttrell pounced on a Tiger fumble at the LSU 9 yard line, and Andridge found Butler with a touchdown pass on the very next play for a 7–0 second-quarter lead. Cafego added a 16-yard scoring run in the third quarter, and Wallen closed the scoring with a 2-yard plunge in the fourth.

A model of consistency, star halfback Bob Foxx scored six touchdowns for the Volunteers in 1938, six in 1939, and six in 1940.

Tennessee 34, Citadel 0: Cafego suffered a season-ending knee injury—but not before tossing an 18-yard scoring pass to Ed Cifers that gave Tennessee a 7–0 first-period advantage. Wallen plunged over from the 1 yard line to open a twenty-point second-quarter outburst that concluded with a 38-yard touchdown pass from Butler to Emil Hust and a 3-yard run by Van Thompson. Newman wrapped up the scoring with another 3-yard burst—this one coming in the third period.

Football— A Game of Inches

Tennessee's 1939 football team was the last major college squad to play an entire regular season without allowing a point—a feat recognized by everybody except Vanderbilt's Roy Huggins.

After holding their first seven opponents scoreless, the '39 Volunteers were in serious danger of losing the shutout streak in Game 8 against Vanderbilt on November 18 at Shields-Watkins Field in Knoxville.

As always, Tennessee coach Robert R. Neyland chose to rest his starters for the last ten minutes of the first half. Operating against second-team defenders, Vanderbilt marched to a first-and-goal at Tennessee's 3 yard line late in the second quarter. One smash into the line later, the ball was on the 1 yard line. With three downs left to advance the ball a mere 36

Tennessee 13, Vanderbilt 0: Tennessee's unbeaten streak appeared to be in jeopardy when the stingy Commodores held the Volunteers without a first down the entire opening half. Warren found James Coleman with an 11-yard touchdown pass in the third quarter, however, and Newman returned an interception 64 yards for a clinching touchdown in the fourth period. Incredibly, Tennessee won without recording a single rushing first down in the game.

inches, the Commodores appeared almost certain to end Tennessee's scoreless run.

Huggins, Vanderbilt's fullback, got the handoff on second down and plowed into a small opening at right tackle, quickly disappearing into a mass of humanity that included sophomore lineman Don Edmiston and several of his Volunteer pals.

After the pile of bodies dispersed, officials placed the ball inches from the goal line, bringing a roar of approval from the partisan home crowd.

"I got in," Huggins would later insist, "but they pushed me back, and in those days they didn't mark it as strictly by forward motion as they do now."

Vanderbilt still had two opportunities to gain a few inches. With Tennessee's defense massed in the middle of the field, the Commodores tried an end-around play to the outside. Several quick-reacting Volunteers swarmed the ballcarrier, however, belting him to the ground at the 5 yard line.

When the fourth-down play also failed, Vanderbilt's scoring threat died. Tennessee eventually recorded two fourth-quarter touchdowns and prevailed 13–0. The Volunteers beat Kentucky 19–0 and Auburn 7–0 over the next two weeks to complete the regular season without permitting an opponent to score . . . Roy Huggins's claim notwithstanding.

Tennessee 19, Kentucky 0: The homestanding Wildcats never had a chance. Bartholomew opened the scoring with a 1-yard plunge. Foxx scored on a 19-yard reverse moments later, as the visiting Volunteers grabbed a 12–0 first-quarter lead. Butler combined with Hust on a 15-yard touchdown aerial, and Thompson passed to Wallen for the extra point to conclude the scoring.

Tennessee 7, Auburn 0: On a day when both defenses seemed impregnable, Johnny Butler's 40-yard punt return and Ike Peel's PAT kick provided the game's only points. Tennessee thus concluded the 1939 season unbeaten, untied, and unscored-upon. In addition, the victory marked Tennessee's fifteenth consecutive shutout, including the final four regular-season games of 1938 and the 1939 Orange Bowl Game.

Note: The Volunteer defense's air of invincibility disappeared and Neyland's bowl jinx began when Tennessee traveled to Pasadena for its first-ever appearance in the Rose Bowl. With Cafego's injured knee limiting him to one brief appearance, the Volunteers could not sustain any offense. They fell 14–0 to the Southern California Trojans.

1940 Season

Tennessee 49, Mercer 0: One of the strangest plays in Volunteer history punctuated Tennessee's 1940 opener. The Volunteers led 14–0 after two periods, thanks to a 4-yard run by Andridge and a 14-yard ramble by Butler. Tennessee advanced to the Mercer 16 yard line early in the third quarter, and then Butler completed a pass to Hust, who bobbled the ball. Foxx recovered the midair fumble and raced across the goal line to complete the bizarre touchdown. Tennessee's scoring trickle turned into an avalanche at this point. Andridge sped 21 yards off left tackle and Max Steiner scored on a 2-yard return of a blocked punt to complete a twenty-one-point third-quarter explosion. The Volunteers then tacked on two more touchdowns in the fourth period—those coming on an 11-yard pass from Thompson to Hust and an 8-yard burst by Elwood Powers.

Tennessee 13, Duke 0: Tennessee made two second-quarter touchdowns stand up in stretching its three-year regular-season winning streak to twenty-four games. Foxx accounted for all thirteen points—completing a 33-yard pass to Hust for the first touchdown, kicking the PAT, and later plowing 1 yard over left guard for the second touchdown.

Tennessee 53, Chattanooga 0: Tennessee registered its seventeenth consecutive regular-season shutout by blasting the Moccasins. The game was little more than a glorified scrimmage as Foxx (14 yards), Andridge (12 yards), Thompson (3 yards and 33 yards), Hust (12-yard pass from Butler), and Fred Newman (2 yards) scored offensive touchdowns for the Volunteers. Tennessee's defense tacked on the last two scores—Leonard Simonetti lumbering 10 yards with a blocked punt and Newman racing 69 yards with an interception.

Tennessee 27, Alabama 12: Down 6–0 in the second quarter, Tennessee took control thanks to some Butler heroics. The Volunteer tailback rambled 68 yards to the Alabama 10 yard line and then passed to Hust for a touchdown on the very next play. Newman's PAT gave the Volunteers a 7–6 lead. Moments later, Butler returned a punt 48 yards for a touchdown, and Newman's kick widened the gap 14–6. Alabama closed to 14–12, but Tennessee salted away the victory with two fourth-period touchdown passes from Warren to Mike Balitsaris—an 8-yarder and a 23-yarder.

Tennessee 14, Florida 0: William Nowling broke a scoreless tie with a 48-yard third-quarter touchdown run, and then Warren added a 49-yard scamper around right end in the final period to nail down Tennessee's twenty-seventh consecutive regular-season triumph.

Tennessee 28, Louisiana State 0: Butler resumed his big-play antics by racing 73 yards on a first-quarter punt return to the LSU 3 yard line and then scoring moments later on a 1-yard "fake pass," forerunner of today's quarterback draw. Foxx had a big day as well, scoring on a 5-yard run and tossing a 35-yard touchdown pass to Coleman.

Tennessee 40, Southwestern 0: Thompson burst 37 yards and Butler 32 for early touchdowns as the Volunteers rolled in Memphis. Warren contributed two more touchdowns—one coming on a 21-yard touchdown pass to Richard Mulloy and the other on a 1-yard run.

Tennessee 41, Virginia 14: The Volunteers built a 34–0 lead and then coasted to a victory that extended their regular-season winning streak to thirty games. Nowling opened the scoring with a 1-yard run and then Foxx scored from the 4 yard line on a fake pass. Newman added touchdown runs of 1 and 3 yards, and then James Schwartzinger bolted off left tackle on a 5-yard scoring burst. Broome added the final touchdown by plowing 3 yards over center.

Tennessee 33, Kentucky 0: Leading just 7–0 at halftime and 14–0 after three periods, Tennessee exploded for nineteen fourth-quarter points to subdue the pesky Wildcats. The first two touchdowns came via the air—Butler finding Balitsaris with a 9-yard second-quarter pass and then Warren hitting Coleman with a 7-yarder. The fourth-quarter blitz included a 26-yard Butler-to-Balitsaris touchdown pass and a 37-yard interception return by Newman.

Tennessee 20, Vanderbilt 0: The Volunteers completed their third consecutive undefeated, untied season with a hard-fought victory in Nashville. Foxx broke a scoreless tie with a 15-yard burst off right tackle in the second quarter. Tennessee widened the gap to 14–0 in the third period when Warren circled right end for a 35-yard score and then concluded the scoring when Butler took a lateral from Newman and bolted 14 yards to pay dirt.

Note: Again showing his mortality at bowl time, Neyland came out on the short end of a 19–13 score against Boston College in the Sugar Bowl. Short touchdown runs by Thompson and Warren gave Tennessee a 13–7 lead midway through the third quarter, but the Eagles stormed back to tie the game. Foxx's attempt to provide a 16–13 lead was foiled when his 25-yard field goal attempt bounded off the upright. BC then scored a game-winning fourth-quarter touchdown on what the scoring summary called "a beautiful broken field run of 24 yards" by O'Rourke. Incredibly, ten Volunteers who began their varsity careers as sophomores in 1938 concluded them in 1940 without suffering a regular-season loss or tie. They were ends James Coleman and Ed Cifers; tackles Abe Shires, Burr West, and Bill Luttrell; guards Bob Suffridge and Ed Molinski; tail-back Buist Warren; and wingbacks Bob Foxx and Robert Andridge.

1941 Season

Tennessee 32, Furman 6: Leading just 7–6 at halftime, the Volunteers erupted for twenty-five second-half points to notch the last of their thirty-three consecutive regular-season triumphs. Butler threw 13 yards to Balitsaris for the first touchdown and hit Hust from 52 yards for the second. Cifers scored touchdown number three on a 2-yard burst and completed a 35-yard pass for number four. Charles Mitchell concluded the scoring for Tennessee with a 13-yard ramble.

Duke 19, Tennessee 0: All good things must end, and Tennessee's remarkable regular-season winning streak came to a grinding halt on October 4, 1941, at Durham, North Carolina. The homestanding Blue Devils struck for all their points in the first half, the final six coming when they recovered a muffed punt in the Volunteer end zone.

Postscript: During their amazing thirty-three-game regular-season winning streak, the Volunteers outscored the opposition 884–48. Only one opponent during this stretch came within a touchdown of Tennessee—Auburn, losing by 7–0 scores in 1938 and 1939. When the streak finally ended, Neyland was not the losing coach. He had rejoined the U.S. Army prior to the start of the 1941 season, leaving the program in the hands of assistant coach John Barnhill. Neyland returned in time for the 1946 season and won his first four games, extending his personal regular-season winning streak to thirty-six games before losing to Wake Forest.

One Tough "Suff"

Quinn Decker was no stranger to football talent, having lettered as a University of Tennessee fullback in 1928, 1929, and 1930. Yet the youthful head coach of Knoxville's Central High School had never seen a prospect who exhibited the powerful burst of the raw newcomer named Robert Lee Suffridge. He wasn't particularly big or strong, but he had such remarkable quickness that he virtually exploded past blockers to make tackle after tackle during practice. Decker knew the dynamic teenager could be a magnificent addition to the Bobcat defense, except for one detail . . . he had not yet graduated from Smithwood Grammar School.

Fingers crossed, the coach dropped by a Fountain City drug store and telephoned the state's high school governing board to request a ruling that would allow the boy to play for Central while still attending grammar school classes. A. V. Goddard took Decker's call, listened attentively, and promised to call back with a ruling.

Robert, standing nearby, overheard Decker's end of the conversation. Desperate to play high school football, he slipped out of the drug store and made his way down the street. Stopping after 2 blocks, he called the drug store and asked to speak with Decker. Granted this request, he falsely identified himself as Goddard.

"Suffridge is eligible to play," he said, disguising his voice a bit. "He can play on your team against Middlesboro tomorrow."

Suiting up for his first high school game the following day, Suffridge found himself thrust into Central's starting lineup. With the outcome in doubt heading into the final minute, he shocked the partisan Kentucky crowd by running down a Middlesboro ballcarrier from behind to make a game-saving tackle that preserved a 6–0 Bobcat triumph.

Celebrating his triumphant debut on the return trip to Knoxville, Suffridge was snapped back to reality when Central's coach summoned him to the rear of the bus. Wasting no time, Decker asked whether the youngster was aware that his eligibility had been questioned.

Feigning innocence, the boy replied, "Why no, coach. Why do you ask?"

"Well, I only asked Mr. Goddard for a ruling on a player, and I didn't give him a specific name," Decker answered. "Yet when he called back, he said that *Suffridge* was eligible."

A short while later, as the bus ground to a halt outside the Fountain City drug store, the druggist rushed into the parking lot and gave Decker a handwritten message that confirmed his suspicions. It read: "Player most definitely would not be eligible—A. V. Goddard."

Suffridge's season ended abruptly that night, but his friendship with Decker did not. Many years later, as head man at the Citadel, Decker would hire his former pupil as line coach.

In the interim, "Suff" would establish himself as one of the greatest players ever to pull on a helmet and shoulder pads—three-time All-American at the University of Tennessee, winner of the Knute Rockne Award as the nation's top lineman in 1940, a member of the Associated Press eleven-man All-Time Team in 1950, a 1961 inductee into the Football Foundation Hall of Fame, and a member of *Sports Illustrated*'s

As a defensive player, Bob Suffridge boasted what head coach Robert Neyland called "the quickest and most powerful charge for his size I have ever seen."

eleven-man All-Century Team honored on college football's one hundredth anniversary in 1969.

Although he was a man among men on the gridiron, Suffridge would always remain a boy at heart. His penchant for mischief and practical jokes peaked in college, when he roomed with another young football star of like mind, James Coleman. The two wreaked so much havoc as Volunteer freshmen in 1937 that their no-nonsense head coach, Major Robert R. Neyland, probably considered dismissing them. Instead he elected to separate them. As the 1938 season dawned, he curtly ordered Suffridge to find a new roommate.

Two months later, Neyland casually asked Suff who his roommate was. When the reply was "Jimmy Coleman," the head coach made no attempt to mask his disgust; he demanded to know why Suffridge had not followed instructions.

"Well," Suffridge replied, "nobody else would room with me, and nobody else would room with Coleman."

Clearly unamused, Neyland huffed, "You two remind me of a couple of cadets I knew at West Point."

Suffridge couldn't resist: "Who was the *other* one?"

Like many other elite athletes, Suffridge excelled in several sports. An accomplished track man in high school, he showed his speed in the 440 run and exhibited his strength by heaving the shot put. He also distinguished himself on the baseball diamond and the basketball court. All these activities, he believed, helped fine-tune his body for the rigors of the gridiron. So did his paper route, one of the longest and most exhausting in Knox County. Delivering those newspapers each day turned his calves into bulging pistons, elevated his stamina to remarkable heights, and further strengthened his resolve. Bob Suffridge would not settle for being an ordinary football player; he was determined to be a star.

Once he rejoined Central High School's starting eleven—this time as a fully eligible sophomore—he quickly established himself as a standout on defense, utilizing his blazing speed to undermine even the most well-conceived plays. Opponents tried to run away from him, but that merely played to his strength. Wherever the ballcarrier went, Suffridge could be found in hot pursuit. At times there seemed to be two of him.

Quick as he was, Suffridge realized that he needed more strength in order to compete with some of the bigger opponents he faced. This problem was solved when Central's line coach, Nathan "Red" Eubank, introduced him to the medicine ball, a ten-pound leather-covered sphere used in conditioning. Intrigued by the possibilities, Suffridge often lugged the ball with him on 5-mile runs, tossing it into the air and catching it as he jogged. He later credited this practice with developing the powerful forearms that made him so effective in hand-to-hand combat with opposing linemen.

With his football career on the fast track, young Robert seemed to have everything going his way. A problem loomed on the home front, however. Brack Suffridge did not approve of his son's passion for football. The two argued with increasing regularity about the pros and cons of the sport. Weary of the seemingly endless shouting matches, Robert left home and hit the streets.

Years later he explained the bold move to biographer Raymond Edmunds, who wrote *Football Beyond Coaching*:

"Dad didn't understand football. He didn't know what it did for young boys coming up. He didn't know the self-respect you gained by making a good tackle or blasting a defensive man out of the way to shake a runner loose. He just didn't understand football. I don't guess I did, either, but I do know that when I tied those shoe strings before a game I went into

Suffridge's college career earned him selection to the Associated Press All-Time Team in 1950 and Sports Illustrated's *First 100 Years Team in 1969.*

some sort of a trance. . . . I felt real big. Just waited for the whistle and then I was in heaven."

Eventually young Suffridge took up residence in the office basement of Dr. Carl Martin. Although Dr. Martin soon began paying him to do odd jobs, Robert assumed that the doctor did not know there was a boarder in his basement. One day, however, Martin asked Robert if there was room in the basement for a mattress and some other household items. The boy nodded and soon found himself in a furnished apartment, rent free.

Freed from his father's resistance, Suffridge continued to blossom as a football player. Although he relished the thrill of tracking down a ballcarrier and slamming him to the turf, he began developing a similar fondness for offensive guard play.

"I found out that it was just about as much fun to block as it was to tackle," he told his biographer many years later. "Down in my heart I always wanted to carry the ball, and I guess I felt like I had the ball when I swept wide to clear the way."

When he wasn't blocking opponents, Suffridge was blocking their punts. In his three years of high school ball, he managed to foil a mind-boggling twenty-nine punt attempts, nearly one per game. Proving to be a terror on offense, defense, and special teams, he guided the Bobcats to thirty-three consecutive victories, served as captain his senior year, made all-state three times, and was voted the state's Most Valuable Player as a junior and senior.

For all his success on the football field, though, Suffridge never quite mastered the art of dating girls. An intimidator in the trenches, he was the intimidated in the clinches.

"I remember one night at church I was walking this girl home and she kissed me," he recalled years later. "I left her and ran all the way home."

Once his high school career was completed, Suffridge considered attending the University of Alabama. Reportedly the Tide coaching staff showed little interest in him, assuming that he was too small to play guard at 6 feet, 180 pounds. Thus spurned, Suffridge elected to remain in Knoxville and enroll at the University of Tennessee.

After playing for the freshman team in 1937, Suffridge moved up to the varsity in '38 and quickly discovered Neyland to be quite a taskmaster. Coming off a three-loss season in '37, The Major was in a foul mood when he assembled his 1938 team for the start of spring practice. Actually, the term "spring practice" was a bit of a misnomer. The workouts began on January 9 and concluded five months later, in June.

"Neyland said he would never lose three games again in one season," Suffridge recalled years later. "He had his assistants in the office by 6:00 A.M., and he was there to open the office every day during that spring."

Practices were long and grueling. Suffridge later admitted that he "prayed for a broken arm." Once the season began, however, he played each game with an almost maniacal determination to win.

"If you smile when you get beat," he once said, "you have no business out there playing. Be mad as hell when you lose, not unsportsmanlike, but be angry. Then you won't lose as much."

That strategy served him well. After winning thirty-three consecutive games at Central, he played on Tennessee teams that went 30–0 in regular-season play but lost two of three bowl games. The 1938 team went 11–0, beat Oklahoma in the Orange Bowl, and ranked number two nationally. The 1939 team went 10–1, lost to Southern California in the Rose Bowl, and also finished number two. The 1940 team went 10–1, lost to Boston College in the Sugar Bowl, and ranked number four. (In those years, the final national rankings were issued prior to bowl season.)

Suffridge played three of his best college games against mighty Alabama. In one outing he spent so much time in the Tide backfield belting All-American Jimmy Nelson that Nelson finally handed him the ball and said, "Hell, Bob, you play tailback. You're back here more than I am."

Suff turned in another spectacular performance against the University of Mississippi in 1938. To motivate their star

Tennessee's Best Game Ever?

Many longtime University of Tennessee football fans insist that the 1938 team was the greatest in school history. That squad breezed through ten regular-season games unbeaten and untied and then walloped Oklahoma 17–0 in the Orange Bowl.

Over the course of those eleven games, the '38 Volunteers outscored their foes by a whopping 293–16 margin—the only opposing points coming in a 26–3 Game 1 defeat of Sewanee, a 20–7 Game 2 defeat of Clemson, and a 14–6 Game 6 defeat of Louisiana State.

Despite this dominating performance, Tennessee finished second to Texas Christian University in the final Associated Press national rankings that season. The Volunteers might have ranked number one, though, if the polling had been done *after* the bowl games, as is the case today. Tennessee's performance against Oklahoma in the Orange Bowl was downright imposing.

The game's first scrimmage play saw Volunteer tailback George Cafego somersault Oklahoma Sooner All-American Waddy Young with a wicked block that set the tone for the afternoon. Tennessee dominated play throughout the contest and won with surprising ease.

If the 1938 squad was Tennessee's greatest team ever, its Orange Bowl victory over Oklahoma on January 1, 1939, perhaps qualifies as Tennessee's greatest game ever. This supposition would have gotten no argument from All-American Bob Suffridge, who anchored the Volunteers' offensive and defensive lines that fateful day.

"George Cafego practically killed Young on our first running play," Suffridge recalled. "Bob Foxx acted like there was no defense against him at all, and Bowden Wyatt kicked a field goal that would have been good from 60 yards out. I made a few tackles myself. Abe Shires was in there raising a lot of hell, too.

"We were great that day, as great as we ever were during my entire career."

player, Tennessee's coaches spent two weeks raving about Rebel standout Parker Hall. The ploy worked; Suffridge was ready to tear the locker-room door off its hinges by kickoff. Early in the game he beat the Rebels' center with a nifty move, flattened the fullback for a thunderous forearm, and then buried his shoulder into Hall's stomach, driving him 5 yards backward and flat onto his back. Hall was helped from the field and did not return to action as Tennessee romped 47–0.

Suffridge had such a quick and ferocious charge at the start of a play that he often seemed to be ahead of the snap count. Eventually Neyland began alerting officials of this before every Volunteer game so that they wouldn't assume the young standout was jumping offsides on every play.

While their stark contrast in personalities generally kept The Major and Suff at odds, the coach developed a deep and abiding respect for his star player's remarkable football skills.

Neyland later wrote: "He was a tremendous offensive guard, using a very powerful shoulder charge, and he was highly adept at pulling from his position and leading ballcarriers downfield, where he was very effective in open-field blocking. Defensively, he had the quickest and most powerful charge for his size I have ever seen. He had a knack of locating the ball and getting through to the ballcarrier before the latter reached the line of scrimmage. Also, he was tremendous at rushing the kicker and passer. He blocked many punts and tackled opposing passers for many disastrous losses."

Suffridge's talents did not include being gracious in defeat. He found Tennessee's 14–0 loss to Southern California in the 1940 Rose Bowl particularly disturbing. He would later grumble that the man blocking him that day, All-America guard Black Jack Harry Smith, was "big, fat and easy. If he was an All-American, our third-team guards were All-World."

Suff's sullen nature on fall Saturdays was in stark contrast to the happy-go-lucky persona he displayed away from the gridiron. In an article naming him to college football's First 100 Years Team in 1969, Dan Jenkins of *Sports Illustrated* wrote: "One needs to say little else of Tennessee's Bob Suffridge except that Bob Neyland considered him the greatest linemen he ever had. Suffridge was a moody, antagonistic player who could hardly eat or speak on the day of a game. Best of the pulling single-wing guards, he was a defensive terror, as well."

Following his remarkable college career, Suffridge was chosen with the forty-second pick in the National Football League Draft. Selected to play in the College All-Star Game against the NFL champion Chicago Bears, he suited up but refused to enter the contest because (1) he wasn't in the starting lineup, and (2) the team that owned his contract, the Philadelphia Eagles, offered him $250 to bypass the game and avoid the risk of injury.

That may have been a wise move, since Suffridge starred as a rookie in 1941. In one game he stormed through the line to block a point-after touchdown but was called for offsides. He promptly blocked the ensuing attempt but again was flagged for offsides. Undeterred, he blocked the third attempt, this time drawing no penalty flag. He did, however, draw a $100 fine from head coach Greasy Neal. Insisting he had done no wrong, Suffridge suggested that his coach check the game film. Neal did so, realized that the rookie lineman was not offsides on any of the three kicks, and promptly rescinded the fine.

Although Suffridge sometimes seemed superhuman, he endured a few excruciatingly mortal moments. He once showed up for a game with Chicago battling the flu and feeling terrible. Reaching the players' gate, Suffridge was approached by a youngster, maybe fifteen years old, who asked to carry his helmet in order to gain entry to the stadium and watch him play. When Suff agreed, the boy expressed his gratitude by giving his hero an apple. The NFL rookie absentmindedly stuffed the fruit into his coat pocket as the two strolled into the stadium.

Slowed by the virus, Suffridge played perhaps the worst game of his career. He missed blocks, missed tackles, and was penalized for jumping offsides several times. Long after his teammates had showered and gone, he somberly cleaned up and trudged from the locker room. Crossing the field, he noticed the boy he met before the game waiting for him near the exit gate. Suddenly remembering the gift in his pocket, he pulled out the apple and took a bite. Quickly spitting it onto the turf, he sputtered, "Son, that apple you gave me was rotten."

"Well," the boy replied, "that makes us even."

After one season in the NFL, Suff was called into the Navy. There he played for the Fleet City Service team and earned roughly $200 per game, a violation of NFL rules at the time. Some of the coaches knew Suffridge was a professional but politely looked the other way, since he was serving his country during a time of need.

Following his Navy stint, Suffridge returned to the Eagles, only to discover that his best football was behind him. Slowed by injuries, he played sparingly, and the team lost regularly. At season's end, the owners polled the players on whether Coach Neal should be blamed for the losing record. Thirty-four players voted yes; Suffridge voted no.

"I think we have thirty-four draft-dodgers and only one football player in this outfit," he grumbled. "That player is me. Coach Neal is a great coach; he can't get out there and play himself, but I would bet right now at his age he could beat most of those gutless teammates of mine. Fire the players and keep the coach."

Ultimately Neal was retained, but Suffridge was not. His caustic remarks alienated his teammates and ended his pro career.

"I was through as a player," he recalled, "but I left with my conscience clear."

After serving a year as an assistant coach at North Carolina State, he rejoined his old high school coach, Quinn Decker, at the Citadel. Unfortunately Suffridge found coaching football considerably less fulfilling than playing it.

"To me," he once said, "telling somebody else how to play is a poor substitute."

The first of Suffridge's postcareer honors arrived in 1950, when the Associated Press named him to its All-Time Team. The elite eleven were Jim Thorpe at fullback, Red Grange and Ernie Nevers at halfback, Walter Eckersall at quarterback, Don Hutson and Ben Oosterbaan at end, Bronko Nagurski and Fats Henry at tackle, Suffridge and Pudge Hefflinger at guard, and Germany Schultz at center.

After a nerve-wracking wait, Suffridge was voted into the Football Foundation Hall of Fame in 1961. Among the seven inductees that year were fellow immortals Glenn Davis of Army and Charlie "Choo Choo" Justice of North Carolina. Suffridge learned of his selection via a phone call from Ed Harris of the *Knoxville Journal.*

"When Ed called and told me I had joined the football greats, I almost cried," Suffridge recalled years later. "It really was the end of the rainbow."

Essentially that was true. Without football as the center of his life, Suff bounced from one occupation to another. His boisterous nature proved to be quite a hindrance. He lost a job as sergeant-at-arms in the Tennessee State Legislature when he interrupted a debate by demanding the floor. He subsequently

Big Blue Made Neyland See Red

Kentucky fielded some excellent football teams during the late 1930s and early 1940s, yet the Big Blue was no match for Tennessee during that period. The Volunteers hammered the Wildcats 46–0 in 1938, 19–0 in 1939, and 33–0 in 1940.

The reason? Payback. No team gave Robert R. Neyland more trouble in his early days as Tennessee's head coach than Kentucky. The Volunteers' border rival to the north cost Neyland perfect 10–0 seasons in 1928 (0–0 tie), 1929 (6–6 tie), and 1931 (6–6 tie).

The 1931 game was particularly galling to Neyland because of the stakes. His team had outscored its previous nine opponents 224–9 and reportedly was on the verge of accepting a Rose Bowl bid when Kentucky spoiled the regular-season finale. Denied the Rose Bowl, the Volunteers settled for a berth in the New York Charity Game.

Apparently Neyland carried a grudge against the Wildcats the rest of his days. "Coach Neyland had had some trouble with them when he first started coaching," Volunteer guard Bob Suffridge recalled. "They had tied him a couple of times and robbed him of bowl bids, so he really made us work hard (preparing for the Big Blue). We were real sharp each time we played them, and we didn't have any problem in beating them."

Following the disappointing ties with Kentucky in '28, '29, and '31, Neyland beat the Wildcats ten times in succession and went 13–0–2 against them for the remainder of his career. The combined score of those fifteen games was 265–26.

lost a public relations job with the Coca-Cola Company when he placed a whoopee cushion (simulating the sound of flatulence) in the chairman's seat prior to a board meeting.

Off the field, Robert Lee Suffridge never quite grew into a man. On the field, however, he grew into a legend.

"He was just the greatest I ever saw," Tennessee teammate Bill Luttrell said following Suffridge's death in 1974. "Players and coaches alike had the same thing to say."

George Hunter, another teammate, agreed. "He was the greatest football player I ever knew, any place, any time. He was the apex. They couldn't get any better than he was."

The Humboldt Giant

T he University of Tennessee's first fall football practice of 1949 was not a lot of fun, especially for a lanky and unpolished freshman defensive end from Humboldt. Time after time, General Robert R. Neyland sent blocking back Jimmy Hahn and fullback Andy Kozar slamming into the raw rookie. Time after time, the veteran Volunteers drove him several yards backward. Time after time, the frustrated freshman trudged back to his position and braced for the next round of abuse.

"Neyland was using me as a blocking dummy," Doug Atkins recalled years later. "Kozar and Hahn kept coming at me two against one and knocking me out of the park. Then somebody would shout 'touchdown' and it started again. I was taking a beating."

The first-year player had dominated on the gridiron at Humboldt High School because, at 6'5" and 208 pounds, he was bigger than anyone he faced. On his first day of college football, however, he was learning a painful lesson: Size alone couldn't offset the power and savvy of players the caliber of Hahn and Kozar. He needed technique, and he was about to get it.

Leaning close, teammate Harold Johnson whispered a suggestion: The rookie was too upright. If he would stay lower and take on one blocker at a time—rather than challenging both at once—he might be able to hold his own. Processing the tip, the freshman nodded somberly.

Doug Atkins starred in football, started one year in basketball, and once placed second in the high jump at the SEC Track Championships with virtually no preparation time.

"I'd had enough, so I did what Harold said," he later recalled. "I finally got around to popping both of them (Kozar and Hahn) on the same play. Before long, I'd hit the blockers and the runner on the same play. That's the day I learned to play football."

A lesson was learned—and a career was launched. Douglas Leon Atkins would go on to become perhaps the greatest defensive end ever to lace up a pair of cleats. A two-time All-Southeastern Conference selection, he was tabbed All-America in 1952. Years later he was a unanimous pick for the SEC's All-Quarter Century team (1950–74), earning recognition as the league's "Player of the Quarter Century." He also played seventeen seasons in the National Football League, starting eight Pro Bowl games. He is the only former Volunteer enshrined in both the NFL (1982) and College Football (1985) Halls of Fame. Perhaps the greatest testament to Atkins's ability occurred at a reunion of the Chicago Bears' 1963 NFL Championship team, when longtime owner George Halas gave him the ultimate compliment.

"Doug Atkins," Halas said, pausing for effect, "I have been in professional football sixty years. And you, sir, are the greatest defensive end who ever played the game."

George Allen, who was the defensive coordinator on that Bears team, agreed. Asked to compare Atkins with former Baltimore Colts standout Gino Marchetti, Allen once replied: "Atkins would eat Marchetti alive."

The irony of it all is that Atkins hadn't envisioned himself as a football player; he fancied himself a basketball star. As a high school senior, he guided his team to forty-four consecutive victories, one shy of the state record. He was so certain his future lay on the hardwood at this point that he tried to renege on the football scholarship he had signed with the Volunteers months earlier.

"I liked basketball better than football, so I told Tennessee I was going to another school," he said. "They told me a grant-in-aid was a grant-in-aid. So instead of changing the scholarship, they said that if I went out for football and didn't like it, I could switch to basketball."

To this day, Atkins retains a note from a Volunteer football aide endorsing his decision to play basketball. "I've got a letter saying, 'We're counting on you for basketball. If you want to play football, that's up to you.' And it's signed by Ike Peel."

Atkins enjoyed the best of both worlds for a while, playing freshman football and freshman basketball during his first year on The Hill. From all accounts, he acquitted himself quite well on both fronts.

"I scored thirty-eight points against Georgia Tech, and our freshman basketball team went 25–0," he recalled. "We had fun on that freshman team. A lot of times we beat the varsity in practice. But a lot of those freshmen went somewhere else."

Fortunately for Tennessee's football program, Atkins stayed put.

Still growing, he measured 6'6" and weighed 218 pounds by the fall of his sophomore year. Starting at defensive end, he helped the 1950 Volunteers bounce back from a Game 2 loss to Mississippi State and win their next ten games. The 11–1 season ended with a flourish, a 20–14 defeat of third-ranked Texas in the Cotton Bowl. The Dunkel computerized ranking service tabbed Tennessee national champion.

Because the Volunteers had played in a January 1 bowl game, Atkins was very late joining the basketball team. He earned a starting job in a matter of days but, with the season half finished and his body seriously banged up from football, he found the adjustment unexpectedly difficult.

"I only played in eleven games my sophomore year," he recalled. "I had a few twenty-point games, but I couldn't switch over too well."

Atkins averaged 9.9 points per game that season, even though head coach Emmett Lowery relied on a perimeter-oriented, fast-paced style of play.

"Back then Tennessee didn't use the center too much," he said. "We had a lot of guards shooting from outside. And I never got in shape to play basketball. The other guys came out in October, and I didn't get out there till January. You get banged up pretty well playing football, especially playing defensive end, so it was tough for me to switch over from football to basketball."

Atkins's basketball aspirations faced another hurdle, one never revealed to the general public. He suffered from asthma, a condition that affected his stamina at times.

"He had it pretty bad," former Tennessee football trainer Mickey O'Brien recalled years later. "Some of the antihistamines were coming out at about that time, so we managed to control it fairly well. He still had to go through some pretty hard times, but he didn't complain about it."

The biggest obstacle to Atkins's hoops career, however, wore a coaching whistle and a no-nonsense scowl. "I think Neyland controlled everything, including the basketball program," Atkins said.

There may be more than a grain of truth to that. Lowery, head basketball coach in those days, also served as one of Neyland's football assistants. Regardless, Atkins always felt he was being pressured to forsake his hoops hopes.

Emmett Lowery, head basketball coach and an assistant football coach at Tennessee in 1950, worked with Doug Atkins in both sports that year.

"I think Neyland discouraged things," he recalled. "When I came back from the SEC Basketball Tournament in Louisville (March 1951), they were practicing football the next day. I got in about 2 or 3 in the morning, so I slept in. When I met the bus coming back from football practice, somebody said Neyland wanted to talk to me."

The message was typically gruff and to the point: "He said I should've told him if I wanted to miss practice," Atkins said. "I don't think they ever wanted me to play basketball."

The General was a little more flexible when the Volunteer track program asked to borrow Atkins for the Southeastern Conference Championship meet one spring. With virtually no preparation time, he high-jumped 6 feet 6 inches to place second, further underscoring his status as one of the country's most versatile athletes.

By the start of his junior year, however, Atkins bowed to the inevitable and elected to concentrate solely on being a star-caliber defensive end. Southern football would never be the same.

By now 6'7" and 238 pounds, he fully deserved his nickname, "the Humboldt Giant." Atkins towered over opponents and teammates alike—not only in stature but also in ability.

Kozar, who had combined with Hahn to spoil Atkins's first practice as a Volunteer recruit, came to recognize that his towering teammate was bound for greatness. "He was strong and could run like the wind," Kozar said. "He could run step for step with (star tailback) Hank Lauricella and anybody on the team for 70 or 80 yards. But he never reached his potential in college."

That probably was because Atkins's intensity level rarely matched his imposing size. When he was properly motivated, however, he was a beast—unstoppable and unblockable—as he proved in a 1952 game against North Carolina.

"Doug had a broken hand, and it was thought he might not play," teammate Mack Franklin recalled. "Somebody on the North Carolina side remarked that it didn't matter; Atkins wasn't too good anyway."

The quote got back to Atkins, putting him in an even nastier mood than normal that Saturday afternoon. Converting Shields-Watkins Field into his own personal battleground, he vented his rage on the entire Tar Heel offense, as Tennessee rolled to a 41–14 victory.

"I guess Doug was in on three-fourths of the tackles that day," Franklin said. "That one game pointed out to me what his great potential was."

By then, Atkins was a senior who packed a muscular 248 pounds on a 6'8" frame. He was a man among men, but he still had some boyish hijinks in him, as he displayed one spring evening.

"People didn't lock their cars in those days, so all you had to do was put them out of gear to move them," he recalled. "Several of us went out about midnight and pushed about twenty cars down the hill and onto the football field. It took us about an hour to get all of them out there. Joe Maiure (a Volunteer defensive back) did the steering, and the rest of us did the pushing. We were all worn out. It was probably the most work I'd ever done."

Fortunately for Atkins—and Tennessee's football future—Neyland never learned who was behind the childish prank. "If he'd found out about that, I would've been in big trouble," Atkins noted with a laugh. "He really got mad seeing all those cars parked on his football field."

Atkins also recalled several "panty raids" during this time but insisted that he wasn't a participant in any of them. "It was more good, clean fun back then," he said. "It's not like the stuff they get into nowadays."

Another of Atkins's favorite stories reveals a lot about his toughness—and his remarkable recuperative powers.

"One time I hit my finger on a helmet and bent my finger back at the joint so bad that the bone was exposed," he recalled. "I stayed in the hospital for several days and wasn't supposed to play that Saturday. My understudy, Tommy Hensley, was supposed to start against Houston . . . got his picture run in the newspapers and everything."

On the eve of the game, Atkins was released from the hospital and did some light jogging. Still, he assumed that he would sit out the Houston game and watch while Hensley played. He was wrong.

"The next day I played every snap, and Tommy never got off bench," he said. "Tommy never let me forget about that, either, even though it was the coach's decision and not mine."

And—make no mistake—Atkins always bowed to the coach's decision, whatever it might be. "He did the talking," he says of Neyland, "and I did the listening."

Atkins's three varsity seasons at Tennessee ('50, '51, and '52) coincided with The General's final three years as a coach. And, like others who served under Neyland, he developed an enduring respect for the man's emphasis on structure and discipline.

"It was well organized football," Atkins said. "You didn't waste no time. Neyland didn't put up with no foolishness. He was probably the best college coach of the fundamentals. That really helped me in pro ball. When I got to the NFL I was so far ahead of the consensus All-America guys in the fundamentals that it was pitiful."

Atkins was far ahead of most pro players in just about every category, including size. Listed at 6'9" and 280 pounds in the Bears' program, he seemed almost a freak of nature, especially

Waking the Sleeping Giant

Atkins was such a dominant force when properly motivated that Tennessee's opponents adhered strictly to a "Don't wake the sleeping giant" approach. Forced to motivate himself, he occasionally relied on unusual methods. Jim Goostree, the Volunteers' assistant trainer during the 1950s, recalled just such an occasion.

"I was on the sideline at the start of one game, when Doug Atkins ran up to me," he said. "He told me he was having trouble getting into the action. Then he pulled off his helmet and told me to belt him in the face. I knocked the devil out of him, right across the chops, and he went back onto the field and played great."

Atkins later admitted that he was a much more productive player when he was in a foul mood. "It was better when I got hit and looked bad early in the game," he said. "Then I could spend the rest of the game getting even."

since his father and mother both stood 5'10½". As a fifteen-year-old high school freshman, Atkins was on pace to be of similar size, standing 5'8" and weighing 116 pounds. He grew to 5'10" and 138 pounds by his sophomore year, then shot up to 6'5" and 195 pounds by the end of his senior year.

Although he was selected in the first round of the National Football League draft by the Cleveland Browns in December of his senior year at Tennessee, Atkins saw basketball as his ticket to some quick cash. Returning to Knoxville following a January 1, 1953, Cotton Bowl loss to Texas in his final college football game, he quit school to join a barnstorming basketball team called the Detroit Vagabonds. To ensure that the team didn't leave Knoxville without him, he spent the night in the lobby of the Andrew Johnson Hotel, sleeping in a chair with "a laundry bag and a cardboard suitcase" at his side.

Shortly thereafter, Cleveland Browns assistant Weeb Ewbank was dispatched to sign Atkins, whom he found playing for the Vagabonds in a small Southern town. Following the game they met at a roadhouse, where Ewbank convinced the towering athlete to sign for a mere $6,800. Ewbank then picked up the tab for the meal, prompting Atkins to joke that his signing bonus consisted of "two cheeseburgers and eight beers."

Once again, football had triumphed over basketball.

"It worked out better, playing football," Atkins concedes. "You didn't play as many games in football to wear you out."

Besides, as good as he was in basketball, the Humboldt Giant was far better in football and would become one of the most dominating defensive players in NFL history.

Legendary Baltimore Colts quarterback Johnny Unitas liked to say that "one of Doug's favorite tricks was to throw a blocker at the quarterback."

And fellow Colt Jim Parker, a Hall of Fame guard, almost quit as a rookie following his first head-to-head confrontation with Atkins—changing his mind only after Baltimore's coaches convinced him that everybody in the NFL wasn't as tough to block as Atkins.

For all his skills as a football player, however, Atkins was not particularly skilled at diplomacy. He worked his way into Cleveland owner Paul Brown's doghouse within two years and was traded, along with another player, to the Chicago Bears for third- and sixth-round draft choices. That may have been the most one-sided trade in NFL history. During his twelve-year career in Chicago, Atkins was a three-time All-Pro pick who helped the Bears notch two NFL championships and two runner-up finishes.

On his good days he could be a gentle giant. For instance, he was bearing down on Green Bay Packer halfback Paul Hornung one time and could have seriously injured him. Instead he gently bumped him out of the play, later noting: "I could have really hurt you there if you hadn't been a nice guy."

On his bad days, however, Atkins could be the most intimidating figure in all of pro football. On one occasion the Washington Redskins were walloping the Bears and apparently driving toward another fourth-quarter score. Through gritted teeth, Atkins told Redskins quarterback Sonny Jurgensen, "OK, that's enough. You've scored enough. And if you come this way again, I'll maim you."

Jurgensen admits that he returned to the huddle "trying my best to think of a play that would be sure *not* to score."

In 1967 Atkins was traded to the New Orleans Saints, where he enjoyed three more fruitful seasons. He received the first-ever Vince Lombardi Award in 1968 for his dedication to the game and called it quits a year later at age thirty-nine. At the time of his retirement he held NFL records for full-time players, having played seventeen seasons and 205 games. In addition, he probably held the league record for knee operations (eleven, including seven on his left knee). The guy was one tough hombre.

"They threw away the mold when they made Doug," Saints coach Tom Fears said. "There'll never be another like him."

Deacon Jones, another of the NFL's all-time great defensive linemen, agrees. He once noted that "if the NFL had kept up with sacks back then, Atkins would be the all-time sacks leader, and it wouldn't be close."

Bill Paid, Then Got a Break

Because he joined the University of Tennessee football program in 1954, two years after Doug Atkins departed, Bill Anderson just missed playing with him. He would play against Atkins as an NFL rookie in 1958, however, and the experience would prove unforgettable.

"Doug helped me get a job in Washington," Anderson recalled. "We were playing the Bears in an exhibition game, and the first time I blocked down on Doug he almost killed me . . . knocked me back three steps and pitched the runner on top of me."

Hoping Atkins might take pity on a fellow UT alumnus, Anderson decided to ask a favor.

"As soon as I could talk, I explained to Doug that I was trying to make the team and that he had his spot secured," Anderson said. "He gave me a break, and all of a sudden I became the Redskins's best blocker."

For all the acclaim football has earned him, Atkins continues to bite the hand that fed him. He feels he was grossly underpaid during his pro career—his top salary as a Bear was $25,000—and he responded to his selection as an NFL Hall of Famer (eight years after he first became eligible) by noting, "Better late than never." He is so chagrined by the celebratory antics of today's NFL players that he snidely refers to their sport as "Clown Ball," adding: "I like to see all the clown work they do—flips, dances, strutting around—and they still find time to play football. . . . It looks to me like they waste more energy *after* making a play than making it."

That's vintage Doug Atkins—quick-witted, sharp-tongued, and mildly abrasive. Of course it's easier to be candid when you're 6'9", 280 pounds, and tough enough to toss blockers at Johnny Unitas.

Simply "The Stop"

Equipped with the latest technology, a skilled surgeon can repair a failing heart. Spurred by a surge of adrenalin, a small child can drag an unconscious adult from a burning building. Blessed with remarkable patience, a mild-mannered homeowner can endure ten minutes of a telemarketer's pitch before hanging up the phone.

Ordinary people sometimes do extraordinary things. No better example exists than the 1959 Tennessee Volunteers. They defined the word "ordinary," compiling a mediocre 5–4–1 record. Yet they opened the season with a stunning 3–0 upset of third-ranked Auburn, ending the Tigers' twenty-four-game winning streak. Three wins, a loss, and a tie later, the Vols would face another of college football's elite teams.

The date: November 7, 1959. The site: Shields-Watkins Field. The opponent: top-ranked and undefeated Louisiana State University. The weather: a nippy 40 degrees. The outcome: unforeseeable, unimaginable—and unforgettable.

The Tigers were coming off a 1958 season in which they had gone 11–0 and won the national championship. The Volunteers were coming off a 4–6 season in which they had fallen to lowly Chattanooga and, even more incredibly, played four quarters without making a single first down in a nationally televised loss to Auburn.

As if the task weren't already daunting enough, LSU was fresh from a 7–3 defeat of third-ranked Mississippi, thanks to an 89-yard fourth-quarter punt return by Billy Cannon, soon to claim the Heisman Trophy as the nation's outstanding collegiate player. The Tigers hadn't lost in nineteen games, hadn't allowed a touchdown in thirty-eight quarters and appeared invincible. Tennessee, on the other hand, had lost just three games earlier (14–7 at home to Georgia Tech), had allowed a touchdown the previous week, and appeared . . . well, considerably less than invincible.

The Vols were seriously overmatched, an opinion supported by the game's statistics. LSU piled up 334 yards of total offense to Tennessee's 112. In fact, Tiger running backs Cannon (122 yards) and Johnny Robinson (115) gained more yards individually than the Volunteers gained collectively.

"Tennessee was only close to LSU in performance for about fifteen seconds of the sixty minutes we played," Tiger head man Paul Dietzel said afterward.

Of course, those fifteen seconds would prove decisive, but more about that later.

A 26-yard run by Cannon (who else?) gave LSU an early 7–0 lead. The margin could have expanded to 10–0 or even 13–0, except that placekicker Wendell Harris missed two field-goal attempts, including a 22-yarder in the third period. Still, seven points seemed plenty, given that LSU's defense had extended its no-touchdown streak to forty periods and Tennessee had managed a meager 38 yards of total offense in the first half.

Dietzel was not content to sit on the lead. With the LSU attack stalling near midfield, he ordered quarterback Warren Rabb to pass. Vol defensive back Jim Cartwright stepped in front of intended receiver Robinson to intercept and then followed excellent blocks by Mike LaSorsa and Cotton Letner to race 59 yards and score the first touchdown against LSU in forty quarters, tying the game at 7–all.

Tennessee's coaches had spent much pregame preparation

time reminding Vol defenders to be alert for flat passes to LSU running backs. Cartwright obviously remembered the warning. "I had a notion they might be getting ready to try it," he said. "It's sort of a safety-valve pass they use when the deep man is covered."

Dietzel termed the interception "a tremendous catch," but second-guessed himself for putting the ball in the air. "If we had been ahead 10–0, that pass never would have been thrown," he said.

But the Tigers *weren't* ahead 10–0, the pass *was* thrown, and the score *was* tied.

Seemingly unnerved by the unexpected turn of events, LSU committed another turnover on the first play of its ensuing possession—fullback Earl Gros coughing up a fumble that Tennessee recovered at the Tiger 29 yard line. Three plays later, the Vols completed their only pass of the day, advancing to the LSU 14 yard line. The next play saw fullback Neyle Sollee rumble into the end zone, giving Tennessee a 14–7 lead and turning Neyland Stadium into a madhouse.

Of course, the game wasn't over, not by a long shot. There was still one quarter of football left to be played, and it would be perhaps the most dramatic quarter in Volunteer history.

Tennessee's defense withstood LSU's next charge, but Bill Majors fumbled the ensuing punt and the Tigers recovered at the Volunteer 2 yard line. LSU quarterback Durel Matherne scored seconds later, narrowing the lead to 14–13. Although 13:44 remained to be played, Dietzel made another curious decision. Disdaining a game-tying kick, he opted to attempt a two-point conversion so that LSU could reclaim the lead.

The two-point conversion—in its first year of use in college football—was so new that Tennessee had neither attempted to execute nor attempted to defend one. Yet as the

Charles Severance, the second Volunteer to belt LSU's Billy Cannon on the celebrated two-point conversion attempt of 1959, doggedly insists that Cannon never crossed the goal line.

Tigers lined up for this two-point try, everyone in Neyland Stadium knew what the call would be: Cannon would get the ball and send his 220-pound body slamming into the Volunteer defense. The question was: Which side of the line would he hit?

"We knew that they would go with Cannon," Vol defensive back Charlie Severance would later recall, "but we didn't know which hole he would head for."

Maybe not, but the well-prepared Tennessee defense had an inkling after studying LSU's alignment.

"We knew from the films that when they ran the sweep to their right, Cannon would move back a bit and Johnny Robinson would move up," Vol defensive lineman Wayne Grubb recalled. "I saw this happen and called the play to Jim Cartwright. They ran the play, and we were there."

Sure enough, Cannon took a pitch and headed around right tackle on a power sweep that LSU had used with devastating effectiveness all day. But this time Tennessee's defenders were ready.

Grubb hit Cannon around the knees, yet the powerful running back kept churning goalward. Severance met him head-on inches from the goal line, somehow holding firm until safety Bill Majors arrived to help blunt Cannon's final surge. That play is known in Volunteer lore as "The Stop" to this day.

"Wayne Grubb sort of tripped Cannon up," Severance said. "I had moved up to where I was at a linebacker's normal depth, and when Wayne tripped him, that gave me the best shot at him. And Bill Majors came up from safety to help out."

Officials ruled the two-point try "no good," and the score stood: Tennessee 14, LSU 13.

LSU fans and players insisted that Cannon crossed the goal line on that fateful play. But for every Tiger who said Cannon scored, there was at least one Vol who said he didn't. "The picture that *Sports Illustrated* ran on the cover the next week clearly shows that my back foot was an inch or two from the goal line, inside the playing field," Severance said. "And

Wayne Grubb (61), Charles Severance (14), and Bill Majors (44) combined on "The Stop" of Billy Cannon, preserving Tennessee's 14–13 defeat of Louisiana State in 1959.

I'll guarantee you that Cannon did not get past that point."

Dietzel adamantly defended his decision to go for two in that critical situation. "We came here to win, not to tie," he said. "If I had it to do over a hundred times, I would do the same thing."

Although the two-point call was criticized as being too predictable, giving the ball to the NCAA's premier player surely seemed like a good idea at the time.

"We would've been run out of the state of Louisiana had we *not* given it to Cannon," said Charley McClendon, an assistant on that 1959 LSU team. "It was a case of letting your best runner have the ball in crucial situations. . . . There was no question he got us to where we were. Can you imagine what would've happened had we given it to someone else and not made it?"

All but lost in the raucous celebration that followed The Stop was the fact that there were still thirteen minutes of football remaining. Those proved to be anticlimactic minutes, however. LSU blocked a punt and moved to the Tennessee 16 yard line, but Cannon fumbled a handoff from Matherne, and the Vols' Jack Kile recovered.

Moments later the Tigers advanced to Tennessee's 40 yard line. But Cotton Letner threw Cannon for an 8-yard loss, and Cartwright made his second interception of the game on the next play.

The Volunteers had to withstand one final LSU charge. The Tigers had the ball near midfield when reserve quarterback Darryl Jenkins was called for intentional grounding. Apparently thinking it was third down, LSU then tried a fourth-down handoff to Cannon that was stopped cold, sealing Tennessee's biggest upset since the 1928 Alabama game.

Although he was blocked out on The Stop, Cartwright was

D as in Defense . . . and Donahue

Jim Cartwright made a couple of interceptions, returning one for a touchdown. Wayne Grubb, Charles Severance, and Bill Majors combined on "The Stop" that preserved the lead in the fourth quarter. They were the obvious heroes in Tennessee's 14–13 upset of top-ranked LSU in 1959.

The Volunteers owed much credit for the victory, however, to an unsung hero—assistant coach Ken Donahue. That's the opinion of George Mooney, Tennessee's radio announcer in those days.

"Ken Donahue had responsibility for the scout squad," Mooney noted, "and with his innate ability to understand offense and defense, he was able to prepare Tennessee's defense to stop a much better football team."

A master of understatement, Donahue conceded that the '59 Vols were fortunate to shackle the heavily favored Tigers and their star running back, Billy Cannon. "We didn't have a real outstanding team that year," Donahue said. "But they were a dedicated, hardworking group of young men. . . . We were highly motivated that day. LSU was undefeated, the defending national champion."

Ultimately the game hinged on one play—Cannon's ill-fated attempt to score on a two-point conversion try in the final quarter.

In typical low-key fashion, Donahue recalled the play in these words: "We just figured they'd give it to Cannon in that situation. He was supposedly one of the better running backs in the country."

That 1959 LSU game stands to this day as probably the greatest upset in Vol history. It would be twenty-seven years before Tennessee would register a shocker of similar magnitude, stunning second-ranked Miami (an eleven-point favorite) by an amazing 35–7 margin in the 1986 Sugar Bowl.

The architect of that upset was an aging but deviously clever defensive coordinator. His name? Ken Donahue.

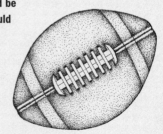

carried off the field by teammates in honor of his two interceptions. He also received a game ball. Everyone on Tennessee's defensive unit probably deserved game balls that day.

"Coach (Bowden) Wyatt did a great job of getting us ready to play," Severance later said. "I think we were as well prepared as we could be. We knew everything that LSU would do, and it was just a matter of stopping them."

With the Tigers trying for a two-point conversion, "stopping them" is precisely what Tennessee's defense did. "If everybody who has told me that he saw that play was really there," Severance deadpanned, "we must have had a crowd of 200,000 that day."

Just as the minutes that followed The Stop proved anticlimactic, so did the games that followed. The '59 Volunteers would not win again. Apparently drained by the emotional win over LSU, they lost to Mississippi (37–7), to Kentucky (20–0), and to Vanderbilt (14–0).

Tennessee finished that season 5–4–1 and unranked, having allowed more points (118) than it scored (112). This was an ordinary team, at best. On November 7, however, the Vols managed to do something extraordinary. They combined for The Stop, the most dramatic play in the most dramatic setting of the most dramatic upset in program history.

Or did they?

Dietzel claimed Cannon "was in the end zone up to his waist."

Wyatt, the opposing coach, readily admitted, "The movies will show that he got pretty close to those two points."

Johnny Majors, Tennessee's freshman coach in '59, was a bit more outspoken: "He damn sure didn't score."

Scooter Purvis, a halfback on that '59 LSU team, elected to be diplomatic: "Cannon wound up, of course, in the end zone. But the official said his forward progress had been stopped."

As for Cannon, he declined comment immediately after the game but later insisted: "I'll go to my grave believing I was over."

And Severance will go to his grave knowing Cannon wasn't.

The Rosebonnet Bowl

W hen Tennessee's offense broke from the huddle for its first scrimmage play of the 1965 Ole Miss game, receiver Johnny Mills muttered "Quack! Quack!" as he trotted to his wide receiver position. It was his custom, a facetious testament to his role as a mere decoy in the Volunteers' run-oriented attack. He even gave himself the nickname "Duck" to underscore the point.

As fate would have it, that first scrimmage play would prove to be the last for Charlie Fulton, Tennessee's starting quarterback. He was injured to such an extent that head coach Doug Dickey was forced to replace him with backup Dewey Warren. Since Warren's contribution in the season's first six games had been minimal, Dickey wasn't expecting miracles. All he wanted from the so-called "Swamp Rat" was a cool head in the huddle. He got his wish; Warren's head was unusually cool. In his haste to enter the game, he left his helmet on the bench. Realizing the mistake upon reaching the huddle, he hurriedly called timeout, and then sheepishly trudged to the sidelines and retrieved his headgear. Not exactly an auspicious beginning.

The Volunteers suffered a 14–13 setback that day—their first defeat of the season—but the game wasn't a total loss. The Swamp Rat and the Duck were about to turn Tennessee football upside down.

Johnny Mills nicknamed himself "Duck" because he was utilized as a decoy so often early in his career. He caught a school-record ten passes in the 1965 UCLA game, however.

The '65 season had begun routinely enough. Although Warren clearly was the better passer, Dickey settled on Fulton as his number-one quarterback because of the latter's rushing skills. Calling him a "knuckleball runner" and Tennessee's "most dynamic player," Dickey once noted: "I hadn't been around anybody with that kind of quickness who could accelerate like Charlie could; he was as quick as anybody out there today for sheer quickness and acceleration and the ability to stop, start, dart, that sort of thing. He was a dandy."

The Volunteers opened the '65 campaign with a home game against Army, coached by Paul Dietzel. On his previous visit to Knoxville, in 1959, Dietzel's top-ranked Louisiana State Tigers had suffered a stunning loss to Tennessee. He fared even worse this time—the Big Orange romped 21–0.

After playing Auburn to a 13–13 tie in Game 2, Tennessee whipped South Carolina 24–3 to carry a 2–0–1 record into its Game 3 showdown with mighty Alabama. The 7–7 tie ended on a surrealistic note when Tide quarterback Ken "Snake" Stabler purposely threw the ball away at the Volunteer 3 yard line to stop the clock in the final seconds. Stabler, who had replaced Steve Sloan three snaps earlier, assumed that he'd made a first down on the previous play. He hadn't, and his fourth-down incompletion squandered Bama's chance to kick a game-winning field goal.

Though lucky to salvage a tie with Alabama—the Tide went on to win the national title that season—the Volunteers were 2–0–2 and brimming with confidence as they celebrated in the postgame locker room.

Their euphoria would be short-lived, however. At 6:53 the following Monday morning, less than forty-eight hours after the dramatic finish against Bama, Tennessee assistant coaches Bill Majors, Charlie Rash, and Bob Jones were involved in a fatal crash. They were only a few miles from campus when a Volkswagen driven by Rash collided with a train. Majors and Jones were killed instantly. Rash lingered for five days before dying.

Tennessee's players, though devastated by the terrible tragedy, voted to play that weekend's game with Houston. Wearing tiny black crosses superimposed over the orange T on their helmets, the grief-stricken Volunteers prevailed 17–8. Then, dedicating the season to their fallen coaches, they shocked seventh-ranked Georgia Tech 21–7 the following week.

After losing both Fulton and the game versus Ole Miss, Tennessee found itself at a crossroads. Seven games into the season, the Volunteers were forced to compete without three of their coaches and their star quarterback. Fortunately, Dickey's leadership, the Swamp Rat's passing, and the Duck's receiving would come to the rescue.

After beating Kentucky 19–3 and Vanderbilt 21–3, Tennessee carried a 6–1–2 record into its regular-season finale against UCLA. The Rose Bowl–bound Bruins carried a number-five national ranking into the game, to be held at Memorial Stadium in Memphis. Tennessee was going bowling, too, having accepted a bid to a relatively insignificant Houston-based attraction known as the Bluebonnet Bowl. No one knew it at the time, but the Volunteers were about to burst onto the national scene in a big way.

Given the fact Tennessee was allowing just six points per game and UCLA thirteen, a low-scoring battle appeared imminent as the Vols and Bruins prepared to take the field on the evening of December 4, 1965. The prospect of a defensive struggle clearly failed to excite West Tennessee fans. A crowd of only 44,495—roughly 20,000 below capacity—showed up for what would prove to be one of the most thrilling games in the history of college football.

The game pitted two outstanding sophomore quarter-backs. UCLA's Gary Beban would win the Heisman Trophy two years later. Tennessee's Warren never won a Heisman, but he won the admiration of his teammates with his folksy charm. A Volunteer assistant coach once noted that "Dewey could walk down the street in front of the athletic dormitory and half the football players would fall in behind him, even if they didn't have any idea where he was going."

UCLA's stars also included Mel Farr, who would go on to enjoy a productive career as a running back in the National Football League, and defensive tackle Terry Donahue, who would return to his alma mater as head coach eleven years later. Tennessee had some budding stars as well, the most notable being center Bob Johnson, plus linebackers Paul Naumoff and Frank Emanuel.

The game began on an ominous note for the Volunteers — Walter Chadwick fumbled the opening kickoff, and UCLA recovered at the 30 yard line. Eight running plays later, the Bruins led 7–0. Tennessee fans must have feared the worst, but Warren gradually calmed those fears by hitting Hal Wantland for 13 yards, Mills for 25, Chadwick for 13, and then finding Wantland for a touchdown on the final play of the quarter to tie the score at 7–all.

The Swamp Rat was just getting started, however. The guy known for saying "I love to hum that 'tater," would get an unprecedented opportunity to do just that. After a 23-yard run by Chadwick, Warren passed to Stan Mitchell for 11 yards and then scored on a 1-yard keeper as Tennessee pulled ahead 14–7. Moments later Dewey was at it again, hitting Wantland with a 26-yard touchdown pass that padded the lead to 20–7 by halftime.

Having pulled two groin muscles during the first two periods, Warren opened the third quarter resting on the Volunteer bench. He remained there while Beban capped UCLA's opening drive of the second half by racing 36 yards for a touchdown that narrowed the gap to 20–14. The Bruins regained the lead moments later. Chadwick again fumbled the kickoff return, and UCLA's Tim McAteer returned it 29 yards to give the Californians a 21–20 lead. When Beban scored minutes later to cap a fifteen-play, 74-yard drive and expand the lead to 28–20, Warren's injured groin miraculously healed. It must have, because he returned to action.

Picking up where he left off in the first half, the Swamp Rat found Mills for gains of 11, 15, and 11 yards. After a sack he again threw to Mills, who caught the ball at the UCLA 17 yard line and lateralled to Chadwick, who rambled another 10 yards before being dragged to the turf. Chadwick bolted into the end zone on the very next play, but Tennessee's two-point conversion try failed, leaving UCLA clinging to a 28–26 lead.

The Vols went up 29–28 minutes later on a David Leake field goal. This seesaw struggle would feature six lead changes, however, and two of them remained.

UCLA pulled ahead 34–29 when Beban scored from the 4 yard line with 3:32 remaining, but a two-point conversion try failed. Following the ensuing kickoff, with Tennessee 65 yards from the Bruin end zone, Dickey called timeout to talk with his quarterback. Instead his quarterback did the talking.

"Don't worry, Coach," Warren drawled. "We're gonna score."

Proving this was no idle boast, the Swamp Rat picked up 16 yards on a throw to Mills, 19 on a pass-interference call, and 20 more on a completion to Chadwick. Three plays later — with less than a minute remaining and Tennessee facing fourth-and-goal at the UCLA 1 yard line — the game's outcome was reduced to a single play.

Dickey's in Demand

Tennessee's thrilling 37–34 upset of Rose Bowl–bound UCLA in 1965 established the Volunteers as a rising program in college football and established their leader as a hot commodity in the coaching ranks. In only his second season as a head man, Doug Dickey finished first in balloting for Southeastern Conference Coach of the Year and third in voting for National Coach of the Year.

After the Big Orange concluded the 1965 season by trouncing Tulsa 27–6 in the Bluebonnet Bowl, Dickey was offered the head coaching vacancy at Oklahoma University. The decision to go or stay was not an easy one. In his earlier days, he felt compelled to go where the jobs were—he and wife, JoAnn, had children born in four different states: one each in Arkansas, Colorado, Florida, and Georgia. Having achieved the status of a folk hero at Tennessee, however, Dickey felt inclined to stay put.

Discussing the Oklahoma opening over dinner one evening, Doug and JoAnn were understandably amused when one of their sons chimed in with an unsolicited opinion: "Well, Daddy, you can't go to Oklahoma because we don't have a Tennessee baby."

JoAnn rectified this situation months later by giving birth to Jaren Anne Dickey. Still, Doug elected to stay in Knoxville, surmising that Oklahoma would be a parallel move. He followed the same reasoning a year later when Michigan contacted him about a head coaching vacancy. Spurned by Dickey, the Wolverines turned to Plan B—some fellow named Bo Schembechler.

After the 1965 Volunteer victory at the Rosebonnet Bowl, Volunteer head man Doug Dickey was offered head coach positions in Oklahoma and Michigan, but he stayed in Tennessee.

No one in the stands knew what the Volunteers' final play would be, but everyone knew what it *wouldn't* be—a pass to Mills. The Duck was out of action, having suffered a broken arm while blocking a few plays earlier. Finding its most attractive option unavailable, the Big Orange had no choice but to rely on Plan B.

Taking the snap from center, Warren rolled out to his left and looked briefly into the end zone. Dismayed by what he saw, he tucked the ball and—pulled groin muscles notwithstanding—began lumbering in earnest toward the left corner of the end zone. Fans held their breath and clenched their teeth as they watched his agonizingly slow quest for the end zone. Finally reaching the goal line at the same instant a UCLA defender reached him, the Swamp Rat lowered his head and wedged his way into the Promised Land with perhaps a half inch to spare.

"There was some debate over whether I crossed the plane of the goal line or not," Warren said later, "but the official said I did, and he's got the vote that counts."

Tennessee's players celebrated the touchdown so unabashedly that they incurred a delay-of-game penalty. Meanwhile, Bruin defenders were stunned. They had never expected that a ponderous quarterback such as Warren, further slowed by injury, would plod his way into the end zone for the go-ahead touchdown. Of course Dewey hadn't expected it either.

"I wasn't supposed to carry the ball," the Swamp Rat recalled. "I was supposed to throw a pass to Hal Wantland but he got knocked down, so I ran it in. They say it was the longest 1-yard run in history."

Thirty-nine seconds remained and, like the preceding fifty-nine minutes and twenty-one seconds, they would be packed full of excitement.

Strong-armed but slow-footed Dewey "Swamp Rat" Warren scored the game-winning touchdown against UCLA on a 1-yard bootleg that seemed to take forever.

First Warren passed to Austin Denney for a two-point conversion, giving Tennessee a 37–34 lead. Then, operating against a prevent defense, UCLA reached midfield on its final possession. With time for one more play, Beban heaved a desperation pass that Bob Petrella intercepted at Tennessee's 6 yard line. Thrilled by his game-saving pickoff, Petrella wasn't stopped by the final gun. Instead he was stopped by Paul Horgan, who stormed off the UCLA bench and sucker punched him near midfield. Having suffered a mild concussion and

The Most Versatile Vol Ever?

His teammates called him George. The public called him Ron. Nearly everyone who saw him play called George Ronald Widby the most versatile athlete in University of Tennessee history.

Widby lettered three times in football, breaking the school record with a 43.8-yard punting average in 1966. He also lettered three times in basketball, earning SEC Player of the Year honors after leading the league in scoring (22.1 points per game) during the 1966–67 season. He is the only Vol athlete ever to earn first-team All-America recognition on both the gridiron and on the hardwood, accomplishing this remarkable feat as a senior.

As if that weren't impressive enough, the 6'4" and 210-pounder led Tennessee's baseball team in hitting as a sophomore in the spring of 1965 and then gave up the sport to earn a varsity letter on the golf team in the spring of '66.

Perhaps the greatest testament to Widby's versatility occurred December 17–18, 1965. He flew to Shreveport, Louisiana to play in Round 1 of the Gulf South Basketball Classic on Friday night. After the game he caught a plane to Houston, where he punted for the football team in a 27–6 Bluebonnet Bowl defeat of Tulsa on Saturday afternoon. Shortly after removing his helmet and pads, he caught a plane back to Shreveport, where he participated in the Gulf South Classic finals on Saturday evening.

As one football teammate noted: "George can do anything."

facial lacerations requiring twelve stitches, Petrella was a bloody mess as he was helped from the field.

Sadly, Horgan's behavior was only slightly worse than that of UCLA head man Tommy Prothro, whose postgame remarks consisted of blaming the setback on inept officiating. "The pro all-stars couldn't have won out there today," he grumbled.

A sports columnist for the *Houston Chronicle* subsequently rebutted Prothro's remarks by noting that "Dewey Warren was the guy who beat UCLA, not the officials."

Indeed. The Swamp Rat shattered single-game school records for completions (nineteen), attempts (twenty-seven), and passing yards (274). Before breaking his arm, Mills tied the school record with ten receptions—not bad for a decoy.

The Duck's performance made a lasting impression on his teammates. As Wantland noted, "He made about ten catches—some of them unbelievable—tipping the ball over his head, diving here and there. Mills was spectacular."

Mills *was* spectacular, and so was Warren. They were so productive in tandem on that fateful evening that Dickey would open up Tennessee's offense in 1966. The result: Warren completed 136 passes for 1,716 yards, roughly tripling the previous school records of 44 completions and 588 yards he had set in 1965. Clearly, the 1965 Tennessee-UCLA shootout ushered the Vols into an era of unprecedented passing exploits. It also qualified as one of the most memorable games in college football history—a classic in shoulder pads.

Dickey called it "a highlight-type game of the era." Even Prothro conceded that "A lot of people who saw it thought it was the most exciting game they'd ever seen."

In an era when many games featured fewer than thirty points by the two teams combined, Tennessee and UCLA had scored more than thirty apiece. Dickey was amazed by the resiliency and resourcefulness his players exhibited. "They just kept coming and coming and coming," he said. "I never saw anything like it. I figured if we held them to fourteen points we might win. I never dreamed they'd score like they did or that we would, either."

Wantland echoed that sentiment, noting that "this game was so wild, it might have been dreamed up by some scriptwriter."

UCLA bounced back three weeks later to upset top-ranked Michigan 14–12 in the Rose Bowl, finishing with a 10–1 record and a number-four ranking in the Associated Press national poll. Meanwhile, a Tennessee team picked to finish ninth among the ten Southeastern Conference schools in preseason closed 8–1–2 and ranked number seven after beating Tulsa 27–6 in the Bluebonnet Bowl.

The '65 season marked Tennessee's return to the ranks of college football's elite. And the unquestioned highlight was that fateful night in Memphis when Warren and Mills combined for a sixty-minute magic show that seems to grow grander with each passing year.

"I've talked to probably 100,000 people who say they attended that game," Warren says. "The stadium only held 68,000, so I guess they must've watched in shifts. I go all over the state, and that's all anybody ever wants to talk to me about. Sometimes I tell 'em, 'You know, I did play in more than one ball game.'"

That's true. He played in lots of ball games. But it was the Rosebonnet Bowl that would secure an everlasting niche in Volunteer lore for the Swamp Rat, the Duck, and the longest 1-yard run in history.

Unlikely Heroes

A s the 1967 football season approached, only Tennessee's most optimistic diehards dared to imagine a victory over mighty Alabama—pinning their faint hopes on strong-armed quarterback Dewey Warren and fleet-footed receiver Richmond Flowers. It would not be this potent 1–2 punch that would bring the Crimson Tide's two-season unbeaten streak to a screeching halt, however. That task would fall to Joe M. "Bubba" Wyche and Albert Dorsey, who collaborated on a sucker punch that Bear Bryant never saw coming.

Then, again, who could have?

Troubled by bad knees, Wyche had been so unheralded as a high school senior in Atlanta four years earlier that he agreed to sign a one-year scholarship with the Volunteers instead of the usual four-year grant. After doing precious little to earn his books and tuition through his first three college seasons, he seemed relegated to another year of obscurity in '67. Sidelined by an appendectomy in preseason, he opened his senior year as Tennessee's third-string quarterback.

When Warren went down with a Game 2 knee injury, however, Wyche moved to second-string. And when Charlie Fulton broke a rib early in Game 4 against Georgia Tech, Wyche suddenly found himself thrust into the lineup. Clearly unnerved, he fumbled the first two snaps from center. Finally gaining his composure, he rallied to complete eight of sixteen passes for 121 yards and two touchdowns as the Volunteers prevailed 24–13.

Dorsey, who arrived four years before as a walk-on from Tampa, was even more obscure, if possible. He was omitted from the senior photo that ran on the cover of the 1967 brochure due to academic troubles that had rendered him ineligible for spring practice the preceding April. He persevered, however, eventually winning his battle with the books and winning a starting cornerback job with some steady work during preseason drills.

Bubba Wyche earned the nickname "World's Greatest Third-string Quarterback" by engineering Tennessee's 1967 defeat of Alabama.

Just as Wyche wasn't Tennessee's best quarterback, Dorsey wasn't Tennessee's best cornerback. That distinction belonged to all-star candidate Jimmy Weatherford, an exceptional pass defender. Weatherford was so talented in man-to-man coverage, in fact, that the Volunteers' defensive coaches decided to assign him the daunting task of shadowing Dennis Homan, Alabama's All-America receiver. The plan was to play zone coverage on one-half the field, with Weatherford taking Homan man-to-man on the other side—a ploy designed to confuse Tide quarterback Ken "Snake" Stabler.

Despite his solid showing in Game 4, Wyche was a bundle of nerves as kickoff time for Game 5 approached. After all, this wasn't a good Georgia Tech team; this was a seemingly invincible Alabama team that hadn't lost in twenty-five games spanning two-plus seasons. This wasn't friendly Knoxville; it was hostile Birmingham, where the largest crowd ever to see a Vol–Tide game at Legion Field, 72,000 strong, was assembled. And, yes, that was the immortal Bear Bryant pacing the opposing sideline.

"The atmosphere was always exciting when you played a Bear Bryant team," Wyche recalls. "It was electric that day. There was an air of excitement, a gigantic stadium, and a capacity crowd."

In addition, there was a national television audience poised to see the Crimson Tide's dominating defense chew up this third-string quarterback named Bubba Wyche. Even Tennessee's coaches were unsure if the unsung senior was adequately prepared for the enormity of the task.

"We tried to impress upon Bubba the need of being ready," Vol aide Jimmy Dunn said. "He went from obscurity to being the most important man in our offense in one play."

Wyche wasn't the only member of the Tennessee program battling butterflies that day. Head coach Doug Dickey had reason to be nervous, as well. Perhaps intimidated by The Bear, he may have outsmarted himself in the 1966 game, possibly costing the Vols a watershed victory. Trailing 11–10 on a drizzly day in Knoxville, Tennessee advanced to Alabama's 3 yard line with less than a minute to play. The ball was nearly centered in front of the goalpost, but Dickey and his staff disdained a field goal; they wanted to win emphatically by scoring a touchdown. So instead of immediately settling for the three-pointer, they decided to take one more crack at the end zone. Getting the handoff from Warren, fullback Bob Mauriello found no hole at right guard, so he veered farther to his right. Smothered by Bama defenders, he was stopped in his tracks. The ball was still on the 3 yard line, but now it rested on the right hashmark rather than the middle of the field. Given the ball's proximity to the goal post, the severe angle seemed minor. It would prove monumental, though, when Gary Wright's short field-goal try squirted to the right and was ruled no good.

Deep snapper Bob Johnson and holder Warren insisted that the kick passed inside the upright, but the official ruled otherwise, leaving Tennessee to swallow a bitter defeat and Dickey to second-guess himself for a full year. "We'd have been better off," he later mused, "if we'd left the damn thing in the middle of the field and kicked it from there."

The legendary Bryant literally and figuratively "walked on water" as he left soggy Shields-Watkins Field that day. Rather than acknowledge his team's good fortune, however, he offered a bit of consolation to Tennessee's placekicker, who thereafter would be snidely referred to as "Wide" Wright. "I don't think their kicker should feel so bad," The Bear deadpanned. "If he had kicked it straight, we would've blocked it."

Regardless, Dickey may have been haunted by that 1966 coaching miscue when he sat down with *Sports Illustrated*'s John Underwood mere days before the 1967 Bama rematch. "It's the kids that play," Dickey said. "It's not me and The Bear slugging it out in the middle of the field. . . . You get to thinking about The Bear being a genius . . . then comes the big think: How can I outguess him? The next thing you know, you're trying to beat him with gobbly-wobble. But you won't. If you win, you'll win doing the things you do best, and that's what we'll be doing against Alabama. We'll forget the nonsense."

Not really. One of Tennessee's key plays in the '67 Bama game was pure gobbly-wobble—but more about that later.

Although Warren's injured knee was fully mended by game day, Dickey decided to stick with Wyche, who had been more than adequate against Georgia Tech the preceding week.

"My knee was good enough that I could've played," Warren recalled, "but Coach decided to go with Bubba. That was fine with me. I really like Bubba, and I was pulling for him. The way he played that day, though, I didn't know if I'd get my job back or not."

With less than one game of varsity experience under his belt, Wyche was understandably nervous as he took the field for Tennessee's first possession of the 1967 Alabama game. "There were some pregame jitters," he said. "I wasn't worried about my performance capabilities, but I was anxious to get that first snap from center."

Apparently so. Wyche fumbled three snaps on Tennessee's opening drive. He recovered each time, however, and somehow marched the Vols 67 yards in thirteen plays. Halfback Walter Chadwick capped the possession by diving into the end zone from the 1 yard line, and Tennessee moved ahead by a 7–0 score. The lead was short-lived, however, as Stabler scored from 8 yards out to conclude a 51-yard drive that tied the score at 7–7.

Tennessee drove to the Alabama 11 yard line moments later, at which point Dickey elected to lift his ban on gobblywobble. Taking the snap from center, Wyche pitched the ball to Chadwick, who then threw a halfback pass to tight end Austin Denney for the go-ahead touchdown. A subsequent 47-yard Karl Kremser field goal widened the Vol lead to 17-7, but the Crimson Tide would not go quietly. Mike Dean intercepted an errant pass by Wyche and returned the ball to Tennessee's 15 yard line. Alabama scored five plays later and, although a two-point conversion try failed, the Volunteer lead had been trimmed to 17–13.

As the final quarter began, Crimson Tide players held up four fingers in their traditional "The fourth quarter belongs to us" gesture. On this occasion, they were being overly optimistic. *This* fourth quarter would belong to Albert Dorsey.

First Stabler threw a pass to Homan that bounced off the All-American's fingertips . . . into the waiting hands of Dorsey. Moments later, Stabler threw a pass that was bobbled by Danny Ford . . . into the waiting hands of Dorsey.

Albert Dorsey intercepted three fourth-quarter passes against the Tide in '67, earning All-America recognition on the strength of that one nationally televised game.

With the game nearing its conclusion, Stabler attempted to throw an "out" route to Richard Brewer. Stepping in front of the intended receiver to intercept was—who else?—Dorsey. To complete the fairy-tale finish, he returned the pickoff 31 yards for the game-clinching touchdown as Tennessee won 24–13.

Dorsey was understandably ecstatic in the postgame locker room, shouting: "It's my birthday, my birthday! Boy, what a present! We beat Alabama and I scored my first touchdown. What a birthday!"

The fact the game had been nationally televised made the previously unheralded Volunteer a shoo-in for National Back of the Week recognition. And based largely on the strength of the Alabama game—the fourth quarter of the Alabama game, to be precise—Dorsey was tabbed All-America at season's end. That represented quite an accomplishment for a guy who months earlier hadn't even qualified for a spot in the senior photo on Tennessee's brochure cover.

"I imagine I wouldn't have gotten half the honors I did if that performance hadn't come against Alabama," Dorsey conceded. "There's always so much attention focused on that game."

Because the Crimson Tide is such a high-profile program, memorable performances against this storied rival create instant legends: Gene McEver returning the opening kickoff 98 yards in 1928 . . . Beattie Feathers punting 23 times for a 46-yard average in the 1932 game . . . Johnny Butler making a serpentine 56-yard touchdown run in the 1939 game . . . Johnnie Jones bolting 66 yards for a fourth-quarter touchdown to win the 1983 game . . . Dale Jones deflecting and intercepting a pass that sealed Tennessee's victory in 1985.

On October 21, 1967, Albert Dorsey joined the ranks of Volunteers who earned everlasting fame by stemming the Tide.

"What he did against Alabama," Tennessee assistant coach George McKinney said, "was like something out of a storybook."

In the ultimate irony, though, the game that vaulted Dorsey to prominence was not one of his better performances. Quite the contrary, in fact. "I had a virus, with a temperature over 100 degrees that day," he recalled. "I played a horrible game, too, the worst game I played all year."

Wyche wasn't horrible, but he wasn't overwhelming, either. His statistics—eight completions in fourteen attempts for 81 yards—were modest at best. But, like Dorsey, he learned that performances against Alabama tend to be magnified. *Sports Illustrated* gave Bubba the star treatment the following week in an article entitled "Wyche Has Moved to More Elegant Quarters." Fondly dubbed "The World's Greatest Third-String Quarterback," he found himself elevated to celebrity status on the basis of one highly publicized afternoon.

"Bear Bryant was a living legend, and playing against a part of his dynasty made the game bigger than life," Wyche recalled. "Alabama hadn't lost in three years, and me coming out of nowhere and playing the most powerful team in college football made for a really dynamic situation."

Making the game even more memorable was the fact that Bubba's mother was present during his finest hour. She had showed up at Legion Field without a ticket but was admitted to the stadium by a softhearted security guard.

Ultimately, though, Wyche's performance that fateful day would be remembered for three reasons: (1) He was a nobody when the season began; (2) he played a high-profile position on national TV against the legendary coach of college football's premier program; and (3) Tennessee won. That last detail was the clincher. Great efforts in losing causes are soon

He Swamped the Record Book

No player in Tennessee's storied football history had a more colorful nickname than Dewey "Swamp Rat" Warren. No player had a more colorful personality either. For instance, he kept a sign on his dormitory room that read: THE SWAMP RAT MAY BE SEEN BY APPOINTMENT ONLY.

Known for his down-home manner and thick Southern accent, Warren was totally unflappable—on the field and off. "I don't worry about a thing," he once said. "If you don't worry, you do a lot better. Maybe I worry a little bit when I have a bad day at practice or a bad game. But I give myself a good talking-to and go back the next day and try to do better."

Warren's famous nickname came from his coach back at Savannah (Georgia) High School, a former Vol named Lamar Leachman. When Warren arrived late and somewhat disheveled for practice one day, Leachman chided, "You look like you just got off a swamp boat. You ain't nothin' but an old swamp rat."

Warren rewrote Tennessee's school passing records as a junior in 1966, yet the Heisman Trophy went to another Southeastern Conference quarterback. "Steve Spurrier (Florida) won it that year," Warren recalled, "even though I beat him statistically."

Slowed by injuries, Warren wouldn't win the Heisman as a senior either. That year it went to UCLA's Gary Beban, who outdueled him in the 1967 opener.

Still, the Swamp Rat left behind quite a legacy. In two-plus seasons as a starting quarterback, he completed 258 of 440 pass attempts for 3,357 yards.

Perhaps the ultimate testament to his skills as a passer came from former Vol head coach Harvey Robinson, then working as a scout for the NFL's Dallas Cowboys. "I've seen every Tennessee passer since 1929," he said, "and Warren is the best. I don't recall anyone who was even close to him as a passer."

From all accounts, there was no one even close to him as a character either.

forgotten, but good efforts in epic victories never fade from memory.

"I doubt if anybody'd remember the '67 game or my performance in it if we'd lost," Wyche says. "You only remember the victories."

Tennessee had more victories to come that season, but Wyche would play an insignificant role in them. Unable to move the Volunteers in Game 6 against Louisiana State, he gave way to Warren, who sparked all three scoring drives in a 17–14 victory. Having reclaimed the starting job, Warren guided the Big Orange to a 38–0 pasting of Tampa and a 35–14 drubbing of Tulane. Tennessee snapped an eight-game losing streak at the hands of Ole Miss by beating the Rebels 20–7 in Memphis and then dumped Kentucky and Vanderbilt to close the regular season with a 9–1 record—the loss having come in Game 1 at UCLA 20–16. The nine-game winning streak earned Tennessee the Southeastern Conference championship, a number-two national ranking, and the berth opposite Oklahoma in the Orange Bowl.

By the time the Vols began their bowl preparations, Fulton's rib was completely healed. Wyche, the offensive hero of the Alabama game just a few weeks earlier, again found himself the odd man out in Tennessee's quarterback picture. He watched from the bench as Oklahoma nipped the Volunteers 26–24 in the Orange Bowl.

"We had all three quarterbacks healthy for the bowl game," Dickey recalled, "and we didn't know who to play. It was a strange year for us."

Strange indeed. The quarterback situation was particularly bizarre. When Warren was injured in Game 2 against Auburn, Fulton had come off the bench to earn Southeast Back of the Week recognition. When Fulton was injured in

Game 4 against Georgia Tech, Wyche had come off the bench to earn Southeast Back of the Week honors. When Wyche struggled in Game 6 against Louisiana State, Warren had come off the bench to earn Southeast Back of the Week.

Assistant coach McKinney conceded that the Vols were "lucky in having reserve quarterbacks (who) accept the necessity for preparation, even though they know chances of them being needed may be remote."

No Volunteer's chances of contributing appeared more remote than Bubba's at the start of the 1967 season. Fortunately for Tennessee, he was ready to perform that fateful day at Legion Field when a couple of nobodies—Wyche and Dorsey—became somebodies by snapping Alabama's twenty-five-game unbeaten streak. That neither enjoyed any subsequent renown is a moot point. Like the one-hit wonders of *Billboard*'s Top 40, this duet burst onto the scene for one fleeting instant never to be heard from again . . . but never to be forgotten.

Peanut the Pioneer

s evening shadows fell over Neyland Stadium, the natives were getting restless. With Tennessee's offense showing no spark, UCLA's 17–10 fourth-quarter lead seemed virtually insurmountable to a disappointed Volunteer throng attending the 1974 opener. Suddenly an eerie hush fell over the assembled multitude, as though all 70,000 observers were struck speechless. Then came a murmur—almost imperceptible at first—that quickly exploded into a thunderous roar.

The cause of the commotion? A spindly young man with a white 7 on his orange jersey had emerged from the tunnel near Tennessee's dressing room and begun trotting toward the Volunteer sidelines.

Condredge Holloway was back!

The sheer drama of the moment was beyond description, almost beyond belief. The heroic return was unexpected but not unprecedented. Julius Caesar probably got a similar response upon his return to Rome. Ditto for Napoleon when he returned to Paris and Neil Armstrong upon his return to Earth. On September 7, 1974, Holloway's return to Neyland Stadium would rank right up there with them.

He had been injured while running a first-quarter option play that ended when he collided with Bruin linebacker Frank Manumaleuna, sending both reeling. Slowly regaining his feet, Holloway knew he was hurt. Upon examining him, Tennessee's trainers thought he was hurt seriously. The preliminary diagnosis was a separated shoulder that would sideline him for the remainder of the season. Helped into a van,

Condrege Holloway never would have been a Volunteer—or the SEC's first black quarterback—if his mom had cosigned a pro-baseball contract the Montreal Expos had offered the 17-year-old.

Holloway was whisked to University Hospital 3 miles away. When X-rays revealed a slight separation that posed no serious danger, he was rushed back to the stadium just in time to make his dramatic return to Shields-Watkins Field.

Probably no one was happier to see Holloway than sophomore backup Pat Ryan. Pressed into service by Holloway's injury, he had lost a fumble that UCLA recovered for a touchdown to forge a 10–10 tie. When the Bruins scored again to go up 17–10, Ryan and the Vols appeared doomed. Once Holloway emerged from the tunnel, however, fans just knew Tennessee's offense would emerge from its doldrums.

Vol head man Bill Battle was so caught up in the action on the field that he never noticed that Holloway had left the sideline, let alone returned to it. So when the senior quarterback grabbed him by the arm and pleaded, "I'm OK, Coach. Put me in," Battle assumed Holloway was trying to overrule Tennessee's team doctor. But when the team doctor confirmed that Tennessee's top talent was healthy enough to resume play, Battle turned to his star and said, "Well, get your butt out there."

The rousing ovation that showered Holloway as he trotted out of the tunnel was duplicated when he trotted into Tennessee's huddle moments later. It didn't matter that he had an injured shoulder. It didn't matter that he had missed two quarters of the game. It didn't matter that his muscles had tightened up from inactivity or that UCLA had seized the momentum during his absence. All that mattered to 70,000 Vol fans was that their conquering hero had returned in time to save the day.

And that's precisely what he did . . . in characteristically electrifying style.

Deftly mixing nifty runs with pinpoint passes, he marched the Vols 80 yards. Such a dramatic comeback could only end one way, of course—with Holloway scoring the tying touchdown. He did so in spectacular fashion, going airborne at the 2 yard line to clear a couple of UCLA defenders. They belted him around the knees, but Holloway acrobatically somersaulted into the end zone, landing head first to tie the score at 17–all. It wasn't a win, to be sure, but it was a remarkable tie.

Orange-clad fans filed gleefully from the stadium moments later, unaware that Holloway had suffered torn cartilage in his knee on the fateful touchdown dive. He would never be the same.

Nursing shoulder and knee injuries, Holloway was transformed from Heisman Trophy favorite to just another run-of-the-mill quarterback. Meanwhile, Tennessee's offense was transformed from lethal to lethargic. Minus Holloway's heart-stopping heroics, the Vols lost three of their next five games. Still, watching his injured field general operate at half his usual efficiency hurt Battle far more than watching Tennessee's record plummet did.

"When he was healthy, not only could you not tackle him; you couldn't even touch that little sucker," the coach recalled years later. "He'd play hurt, and you could see the pain on his face, and yet he'd stay in the game."

By the time a 28–6 homefield loss to Alabama dropped Tennessee's record to 2–3–1, many Volunteer fans had turned on Battle. Yet he was far more intent on protecting his quarterback than protecting his job. Knowing Holloway held a promising future in pro baseball, Tennessee's head man offered him an opportunity to sit out the remaining games to save wear and tear on his battered body. Holloway politely declined.

Days later, he would orchestrate one of the most dazzling plays in Volunteer history.

He Lost His Teeth but Won the Game

Condredge Holloway was Tennessee's star player in 1973, but he was upstaged on at least one occasion that fall. That occurred October 6, when teammate Eddie Brown turned in one of the most incredible performances ever by a Vol defensive back.

Playing unranked Kansas in Memphis, the ninth-ranked Volunteers found themselves on the short end of a 21–7 score. Brown then ignited a spectacular comeback. He blocked a field-goal attempt with his chin, dislodging three front teeth that he subsequently found embedded in his bloody mouthpiece.

Brown also returned an interception 74 yards to set up a touchdown, returned a punt 48 yards, and recovered a fumble. When Kansas scored a late touchdown to pull within 28–27, the Jayhawks disdained a tie and elected to attempt a two-point conversion. Quarterback David Jaynes's potential game-winning keeper was stopped short of the goal line by a host of Volunteers—led, of course, by Brown.

Brown was named National Back of the Week for the performance.

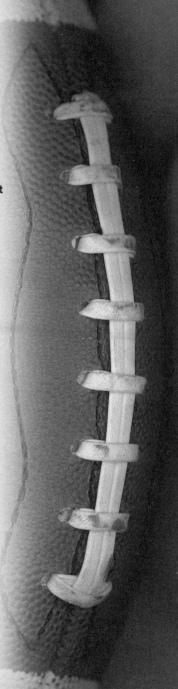

October 26, 1974, was a bright, sunny day in Knoxville, yet hundreds of Tennessee fans were more intent on *selling* tickets than buying them outside Neyland Stadium that afternoon. The prospect of watching two unranked teams, Tennessee and Clemson, was bad news for scalpers but great news for fans without season tickets eager for any opportunity to watch their beloved Vols in person. The matchup was so unappealing to some boosters that they were selling their tickets for a dollar each. Given the game's unforgettable finish, those who paid this bargain-basement price would've gotten a deal at one hundred times that price.

Trailing 28–21 late in the fourth quarter, Tennessee scored in the final minute to pull within a point at 28–27. Since the season already was a disappointment, Battle knew that a tie would do little to appease frustrated fans. There was no doubt in his mind: The Vols had to go for two points.

The call was a play the Vols had used successfully earlier in the game: Holloway would roll out to his right on the pass/run option and look for his favorite receiver, lanky Larry Seivers. If Seivers was open, Holloway would toss him the football. If not, Holloway would tuck the ball and try to run it into the end zone himself.

As officials spotted the ball on the 3 yard line, everyone in Neyland Stadium knew what play Tennessee would be running . . . including the entire Clemson defense.

After calling the play in the huddle, Holloway gave Seivers some additional information: If the Vol quarterback should be stopped shy of the goal line, he would purposely fumble the ball forward into the end zone. Seivers needed to be alert for an intentional fumble.

Alas, Holloway would never get close enough to the goal line to fumble, intentionally or otherwise. Upon taking the

Blessed with great speed and remarkable moves, Holloway's scrambling ability made him perhaps the most electrifying player in Volunteer history.

snap and rolling to his right, he found a half-dozen Tiger defenders rapidly closing in on him. Noting Seivers blanketed in the right corner of the end zone, he shouted, "Larry, go the other way!"

Seivers did just that . . . and so did Holloway. Stopping abruptly, the trapped quarterback quickly reversed his field and began circling to his left. He had retreated all the way back to the 22 yard line when he recognized two noteworthy developments: (1) Seivers was relatively open in the back of the end zone, and (2) a hard-charging Clemson defender was one step from belting Holloway to the turf.

Summoning all his strength, Holloway heaved the ball—the pass leaving his right hand a mere instant before the Tiger hammered him. The ball sailed toward the back of the end zone on a journey that anxious Volunteer fans surely thought spanned minutes rather than seconds. As the pass approached, the 6'4" Seivers leaped, as did a smaller Clemson defensive back. When they came down, Seivers had the ball—and Tennessee had a dramatic 29–28 victory. In an otherwise inconsequential game, Holloway and Seivers had collaborated on one of the most memorable moments in Big Orange history.

Of course memorable moments were Condredge Holloway's trademark, all the way back to age three. That's when he stunned his neighbors in Huntsville, Alabama, by making a shot using an adult basketball on an adult goal at halftime of a game at Alabama A&M, where his dad was a teacher and coach. Given this auspicious initiation into the world of sports, it was little wonder that Holloway would develop into one of America's premier athletes.

By the time he was a senior at Lee High School, he was arguably the most sought-after athlete in America. He could have signed a basketball scholarship with UCLA's John Wooden. He could have signed a football scholarship with Alabama's Bear Bryant. He could have signed a baseball contract with the Montreal Expos, who had selected him with the fourth overall pick in the June 1971 amateur draft. Given so many attractive options, what would he do?

"If I'd been twenty-one years old when I was drafted, I would've been playing baseball," he recalls.

But he wasn't twenty-one; he was seventeen. And in the state of Alabama, that meant a parent had to cosign in order for him to play a professional sport. Dorothy Holloway, who had reared Condredge by herself following her divorce from his

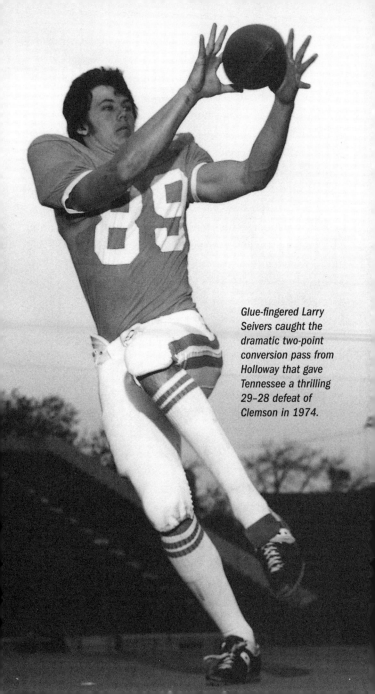

Glue-fingered Larry Seivers caught the dramatic two-point conversion pass from Holloway that gave Tennessee a thrilling 29–28 defeat of Clemson in 1974.

father eleven years earlier, was not about to let her son bypass college in order to play pro ball.

"I'm more concerned with his future than with right now," said Dorothy, who held a master's degree and fully appreciated the value of higher education.

Condredge was convinced that baseball was his best sport, and there is strong evidence suggesting he was correct. The Topps Baseball Card Company named an extra player—ten instead of the usual nine—to its High School All-America team in 1970. This was the only way Topps could accommodate two standout shortstops—Holloway and Robin Yount, who would go on to become a Major League Baseball star with the Milwaukee Brewers. Still, Dorothy Holloway's unwillingness to cosign Condredge's pro contract effectively closed the door on that option.

With his best sport out of the picture, Holloway turned to his second best, football. He was flattered by the interest from Bear Bryant but turned off by the Tide's reluctance to offend the racial sensitivities of a large segment of Bama faithful.

"I had a very vivid conversation with the people at Alabama, and they made it clear that I wasn't going to play quarterback at Alabama," Holloway recalled. "Bear told me I couldn't play quarterback, that they just weren't ready for that at Alabama."

Unwilling to play another position, Holloway began looking outside the state. A program that quickly caught his eye was the Tennessee Volunteers. Their head coach, Bill Battle, possessed the youthful energy and idealism to challenge the racial climate of the time.

"Bill Battle said I could play quarterback," Holloway recalled, "and that was the end of the conversation."

That was the end of the conversation with the Volunteers—but not the end of the conversation with the Montreal

Expos. The Major League Baseball franchise continued to pursue Holloway with remarkable zeal. At one point the club even suggested he take his mom to court in an effort to force her to cosign his contract. He wisely declined.

"How are you going to win that one?" he noted years later. "If you win, you lose; if you lose, you lose."

Still, the Expos would not accept defeat. Mere days before Holloway was to begin preseason football drills at Tennessee, Montreal scout Mel Didier showed up in Huntsville to make a last-ditch appeal. Vol football assistant Ray Trail, who had recruited Holloway, also attended the meeting. The climax of the evening occurred when Didier dramatically opened a briefcase, revealing more money than Holloway had ever seen; estimates range from $70,000 to $100,000.

"I can give you this money legitimately," Didier said. "Tennessee can't do that."

The ploy failed miserably. Holloway was so unnerved by the blatant attempt to buy his loyalty that, moments later, he confided to Trail: "Coach, I'm ready to go to Tennessee."

Holloway's arrival created quite a stir in Knoxville, even though he was so small (5'9", 155 pounds) that school officials fudged and listed him 5'11" and 171. Regardless, he was big enough to guide the 1971 Volunteer freshman team to a 5–0 record, capped by a 30–13 pasting of Notre Dame's freshmen. That game drew an amazing 31,300 fans to Neyland Stadium and showcased two touted quarterbacks, Holloway and the Irish's Tom Clements, who would later become teammates in the Canadian Football League.

Despite his enormously successful freshman campaign, Holloway reported for varsity service in 1972 desperately needing one assurance. He got it.

"Coach Battle said, 'If you're the best quarterback on our

Landing Holloway Was a Real Battle

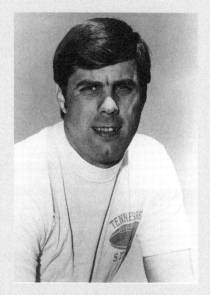

A series of unlikely events had to occur for Condredge Holloway to wind up playing football for the University of Tennessee Vols.

First his mother refused to cosign a contract so that her underage son could join Major League Baseball's Montreal Expos. Then the coaches at Alabama and Auburn had to tell him their schools were not ready for a black quarterback. That forced Holloway to look out of state for a college coach willing to give an African American the opportunity to run his offense.

Vol head man Bill Battle offered Condredge Holloway a chance to play quarterback, a leadership role other Southern schools weren't ready to give to an African American.

He found such a man in Bill Battle, who made his way to UT through equally unusual circumstances.

A tragic auto wreck in 1965 claimed the life of three Vol assistant coaches, including Bob Jones. Following the season, head man Doug Dickey tried to fill Jones's spot by hiring Jerry Elliott away from Auburn. When Elliott declined the job, Dickey hired Battle. Four years later, when Dickey left to become head man at Florida, Battle was elevated to head coach.

Had any of these events taken a different turn, Condredge Holloway might never have become a Volunteer.

team, you can play quarterback for Tennessee,'" Holloway recalled. "After that, everything else was secondary."

Well . . . almost. When he won the starting job with a strong preseason showing, the press began emphasizing the race angle. He was, after all, about to become the Southeastern Conference's first black quarterback. That made Condredge, whom Battle affectionately dubbed "Peanut," something of a pioneer—a mantle that made him uncomfortable.

"As far as being the SEC's first black quarterback, I never viewed it from that perspective," he notes. "It was something that happened because that was the way of the world back then. We played at 1:30 that day (September 9, 1972), and that night there was a second black quarterback that played, Melvin Barkum of Mississippi State. By happenstance, I was first and people made a big deal of it.

"It was historic, I guess, but I never looked at it from that point of view. Trust me, when I lined up against Georgia Tech that day, the furthest thing from my mind was, 'Boy, I'm going to be the first black quarterback in Southeastern Conference history.' What *was* on my mind was trying to figure out whether Georgia Tech was playing zone or man-to-man coverage, then making sure I got the snap from center. The main thing I felt was jitters, like any other sophomore would playing on ABC national television."

If Holloway was suffering from jitters, they didn't show. He debuted by guiding the Vols to a 34–3 dismantling of Tech, which, as fate would have it, was led by a black quarterback named Eddie McAshan.

Condredge led the Big Orange to a 10–2 record that season, earning Sophomore of the Year recognition in the SEC. He expanded his legion of fans in the 1973 opener, earning National Back of the Week honors by rallying the Vols

One Toe-Tapping Tennessee Tune

Bob Neyland was such a brilliant football coach that he had a street and a stadium named after him. But he never had a song written about him. Condredge Holloway did. Holloway was so popular during his stint as Volunteer quarterback that diehard Tennessee fans Ted Goodman and Ray Martin chose to immortalize him in song prior to his junior season of 1973.

"Go Holloway," recorded by a group known as Johnny Vol and the Orange Peels, was released on the Dogwood label and came wrapped in orange and white. The song made thousands of Big Orange fans smile as it blared from their car radios.

Here are the lyrics:

"He was a high school whiz down in Huntsville, Ala-bam
And every coach in the country was fighting to nail him down.
But when the battle was over his mamma said the trail is clear,
'Son go with a winner . . . be a Tennessee Volunteer.'
The Bear thought he had him but he slipped right out of his hand.
He said I love Alabama but The Bear's just not my man.
He left him holding his big uniform,
Said, 'I'm going off to Tennessee and I'm gonna lead the Big Orange.'"

Chorus

"So go Holloway . . . go Volunteers.
The Big Orange takes the field and everyone cheers.
John Ward on the radio play-by-play . . . Bobby Denton on the big P.A.
Shouting 'whooo-eeeee, give 'em six, there goes Holloway.'"

"Jordan said we can beat 'em if we can just steal their signs,
But I believe Holloway makes 'em up at the scrimmage line.
You can rush Holloway, you can trap him, but he won't stop,
He'll go down the middle, around or over the top.
Dooley called him Trickey-Dickey, the master of make-believe,
Said I need a new trick that they hadn't seen at Tennessee.
And The Bear keeps looking, searching for a miracle play,
He might walk on water but he can't stop Holloway."

past Duke 21–17. He scored one touchdown on a spectacular 49-yard run. Then, on fourth-and-4 in the final minute, he set up the game-winner by catapulting himself from the 5 yard line to the 1 to elude a host of Blue Devil defenders.

Still, many observers feel his greatest performance came later that season against Georgia Tech, the team he had frustrated in his collegiate debut one year earlier. On consecutive series, he broke five tackles before launching a touchdown pass to fullback Bill Rudder and then broke six tackles on a 20-yard touchdown scramble that nailed down a 20–14 victory. Performances such as this earned him the nickname the "Artful Dodger," along with the respect of Georgia Tech assistant coach Bill Pace.

"Sometimes I think it's better to just go ahead and let him run the play he wants to," Pace said. "It's when you stop it and he has to do something else that he hurts you the most."

Battle, who routinely described Holloway as "indescribable," knew better than anyone that the soft-spoken quarterback was something special in shoulder pads.

"I didn't really appreciate Condredge's quickness until he dropped by the field after baseball practice (in the spring of '74) and stood in for a few plays," the head man once said. "Afterward, everything else seemed to be moving in slow motion."

Vol aide Jim Wright went even further, noting that Holloway is "so good he can rise above our coaching."

The late Bob Woodruff, Tennessee's athletics director during the 1970s and early 1980s, was another card-carrying member of the Artful Dodger's fan club.

"When Holloway is in the game," Woodruff once said, "you know all sorts of things are going to happen . . . and most of them will be good."

Most of them *were* good. A few were truly unforgettable. No better example exists than that scintillating two-point conversion pass to Seivers in '74 . . . when a one-dollar ticket bought a million-dollar memory.

Johnny Comes Marching Home

Johnny Majors and his wife, Mary Lynn, gazed out the window of their room at the Hyatt Regency in New Orleans, peering with equal parts amusement and amazement at the bedlam in the streets below. It was New Year's Day—always a zany occasion in the Big Easy—but there was something noticeably different on this first afternoon of 1986. Thousands among the celebrating masses were decked out in garish orange hats, orange sweaters, orange shirts, orange pants . . . or all of the above.

The Tennessee Volunteers hadn't won a Southeastern Conference title since 1969 and hadn't earned a bid to a major bowl game since 1970. So when the Big Orange accomplished both feats in the fall of 1985, its fans finally had an excuse to engage in unbridled revelry. It didn't matter that the Vols suffered a loss and two ties on their way to New Orleans. It didn't matter that second-ranked Miami, installed as an eleven-point favorite, was clearly superior in terms of talent. It didn't matter that the Hurricanes were led by future Heisman Trophy winner Vinny Testaverde, whereas the Vols were quarterbacked by an obscure second-stringer named Daryl Dickey.

All that mattered was that this was New Year's Day in New Orleans, and long-suffering Tennessee fans finally had something worth celebrating. Turning from the window to face her

A master motivator, Johnny Majors once spiced up practice by taking a few snaps at quarterback. He went 116-62-8 in sixteen years as coach.

husband, Mary Lynn said, "It looks like an invasion. Like an orange army."

And that's precisely what it was—an orange army on its way to a massacre. Of course the oddsmakers had predicted a massacre; they just picked the wrong troops to prevail. Playing a near-perfect game, the Volunteers spotted Miami an early 7–0 lead and then dominated the rest of the way en route to a mind-boggling 35–7 triumph.

No one was more surprised by the outcome than Majors himself. After watching films of Miami's regular-season games, he and his staff recognized that the Hurricanes were one of the finest college football teams ever assembled. They recognized that Testaverde was unstoppable when given ample time to hone in on his intended receiver. They recognized the enormity of the task before them. So while Vol fans were turning New Orleans on its ear, Vol coaches were turning in long hours at the office. They watched loads of film. They invented new ways to put pressure on the talented Testaverde. And, truth be told, they probably crossed their fingers and said a prayer or two. On paper the game appeared to be a colossal mismatch. Fortunately for Tennessee, this game would be played on a lined field, not on lined paper.

A football squad is made up of many parts—the quarterback, the ballcarriers, the blockers, the pass catchers, the defensive linemen, the linebackers, the secondary, the kick coverage teams, and the kick return teams. To play winning football, a squad needs at least half these parts to be working efficiently. To play a near-perfect game, a team needs the kind of magic that the Tennessee Vols unleashed on January 1, 1986.

"It's all the components coming together," Majors explained years later. "Ours all came together in this game."

Not immediately, though. When Testaverde hit future NFL great Michael Irvin with an 18-yard touchdown pass to give Miami an early 7–0 lead, many among the 77,432 gathered inside the Louisiana Superdome figured the rout was on. They were right—but the guys in orange would not be the victims.

Dickey hooked up with tight end Jeff Smith on a 6-yard touchdown pass that tied the score in the second quarter. Vol receiver Tim McGee recovered a fumble in the Tennessee end zone later in the period to give the Big Orange a 14–7 halftime lead that sent Vol fans into a state of ecstasy. Fullback Sam Henderson bulled over from a yard out to widen the gap to 21–7 in the third quarter, and track man Jeff Powell sprinted 60 yards for another touchdown moments later as the lead swelled to 28–7. Charles Wilson tacked on a 6-yard scoring run in the final quarter, sealing the most convincing bowl victory in Tennessee's storied football history.

The Hurricane warning had been in error. This particular evening belonged to an overachieving but always-believing band of Volunteers.

If Johnny and Mary Lynn thought the celebrating in New Orleans was rowdy *before* the game, they would need an unabridged dictionary to find suitable adjectives to describe the atmosphere *after* the game. Bourbon Street and all its tributaries were awash in a sea of orange. And this time the fans were even louder than their attire.

Poll voters tabbed Tennessee number four in the national rankings, despite an unimposing 9–1–2 record. Majors would later note that "the teams that finished ahead of us had slightly better overall records. But on January 1, 1986, Tennessee was as good as any university football team in the nation."

Although the Volunteers didn't win the national championship that season, they were the toast of college football—and Johnny Majors was the toast of Tennessee.

Again.

Long before he was Johnny Majors, Tennessee football coach, he had been Johnny Majors, Tennessee football player.

Born into a football family on May 21, 1935, at Lynchburg, Tennessee, John Terrill Majors swapped his rubber pacifier for a rubber football at an early age. His father, Shirley, was the head coach at nearby Huntland High School, and all four of John's brothers would follow him onto the gridiron—Bill and Bobby to Tennessee, Joe to Florida State, and Larry to the University of the South (Sewanee).

As a fourteen-year-old freshman, Johnny began his high school career on an inauspicious note—throwing several interceptions as Lynchburg High lost its 1949 opener to Manchester 58–0. He was so snakebit that season that when he finally scored his first prep touchdown—returning an interception from his defensive end spot—his mother missed the play while changing Bobby's diapers back at the family car.

Lynchburg lost every game that year until its season finale. Johnny scored two touchdowns to spark a 19–13 defeat of Huntland High, the school coached by his father. Determined not to lose any more games because of his sons, Shirley moved the family to Huntland so that Johnny would be playing for him in 1950, not against him. The pairing would prove just about unbeatable; Huntland lost just one game over the next three years, and Johnny "Drum" Majors led the state in scoring each season.

Despite his glowing high school credentials, Majors was a bit surprised to be offered a scholarship by the University of Tennessee. He shouldn't have been; a lot of kids got them in those days. He was one of 127 freshmen head coach Robert R. Neyland brought in to rebuild a program that had slipped a bit after winning the NCAA title two years earlier in 1951. Majors would never play for "The General," however. Failing health led Neyland to assume the athletic director duties, handing the coaching reins to Harvey Robinson (1953), who soon gave way to Bowden Wyatt (1955).

Majors lost his nickname once he reached the college level, and understandably so. At 144 pounds, he looked more like a drumstick than a drum. He possessed good speed, shifty

moves, a strong leg, and an abundance of savvy, however, and these traits eventually enabled him to become the country's premier triple-threat tailback—adept at running, passing, and punting the ball.

In his college debut, Majors came off the Volunteer bench to make an electrifying 81-yard touchdown run against Mississippi State, finishing the day with twelve carries for 95 yards. He posted his first 100-yard performance a week later against Duke, rushing twenty-one times for 109 yards.

Elevated to starting status in 1955, Majors blossomed. He ran for 120 yards against Chattanooga and 117 against Alabama and then turned in his first 100-yard passing game against Vanderbilt, completing eight of thirteen attempts for 131 yards and two touchdowns.

He opened 1956 in similar fashion, completing eight of eleven passes for 118 yards and two touchdowns against Auburn. His best rushing games came against Duke (seven carries for 105 yards) and Kentucky (twenty-three carries for 143 yards, two touchdowns). Still, the highlight of that season probably was the Tennessee–Georgia Tech game at Grant Field. The defenses dominated play, but Majors punted brilliantly in helping third-ranked Tennessee upset second-ranked Tech 6–0 in a showdown some observers rank among the greatest football games ever played.

Both opposing coaches that day were Neyland protégés— Wyatt and Tech's Bobby Dodd—and both subscribed to The General's philosophy that defense and the kicking game are the keys to victory. That's why, facing fourth-and-3 at the Vol 28 yard line in the first half, Tech elected to punt. Questioned

Majors reported to Tennessee as a spindly freshman, and left four years later as a celebrated All-American.

later as to why Dodd hadn't gone for the first down, Wyatt curtly replied, "Hell, he wouldn't have made it."

The defeat of Tech moved Tennessee to number one in the national rankings, but the Volunteers' stay at the top was brief. They slipped to number two (behind Oklahoma) after beating Ole Miss the following week and remained there, even as season-ending victories over Kentucky and Vanderbilt pushed their record to 10–0.

In addition to his skills as a runner, passer, and punter, Majors possessed tremendous confidence and a take-charge attitude that served him well as the leader of Tennessee's offense. Teammate Frank Kolinski recalls: "There was no question about who was in charge when he was on the field. Even though he was only 165 pounds, he was the boss. We looked up to him to get the job done. He was Tennessee football in 1956."

Majors' final college game would be memorable in a forgettable kind of way. He fumbled a punt that set up Baylor's winning score, as the Bears tripped Tennessee 13–7 in the Sugar Bowl on January 1, 1957. Fortunately he drew considerable comfort from his mother, who tenderly reminded him that "Everybody burns the biscuits once in a while."

Tennessee fans weren't quite so philosophical. Weeks later, making a public speaking engagement in Kingsport, Johnny offered to hold a one-year-old girl while her father greeted some friends. Nodding toward the stranger holding the little girl, one of the friends asked his identity. When the man replied, "Johnny Majors," the friend wisecracked, "Aren't you afraid he'll drop her?"

Although he was a two-time Southeastern Conference Most Valuable Player and the Heisman Trophy runner-up to Notre Dame's Paul Hornung in 1956, Majors drew modest

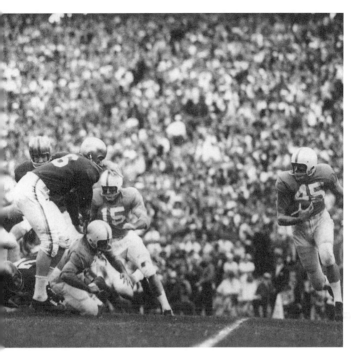

Johnny Majors (45) was such a triple-threat performer for Tennessee in 1956 that he finished runner-up to Notre Dame's Paul Hornung for the Heisman Trophy.

interest from National Football League teams. At 5'10" and 165 pounds, he seemed too small and brittle for the rigors of the NFL. And having played single-wing tailback in college, he was a man without a position in the pros. Given all of this, he elected not to wait for the NFL draft. Instead he accepted a $10,000 contract (plus a $1,000 signing bonus) to join the Montreal Alouettes of the Canadian Football League.

Playing halfback on offense and safety on defense, Majors quickly found his lack of heft a hindrance even in the CFL. He was not allowed to field punts, although he had runbacks of 79 and 69 yards at Tennessee. There was no fair-catch rule in the CFL, making it somewhat hazardous duty. And since Canadian teams were limited to twelve Americans on their roster, most used Canadian-born players on punt returns because they were more expendable.

As injuries caused Majors to spend more time in the training room and less time in the huddle, his role on the team dwindled. Soon he was returning punts, a painful illustration of just how expendable he had become. Cut at midseason due to injuries, he returned to Knoxville and joined Tennessee's staff as freshman running backs coach. With no full-time jobs available, he basically was placed on scholarship again—living at East Stadium Dorm with free meals and tuition while he completed his degree requirements.

Elevated to full-time staffer in January 1958, Majors had no specific duties. He spent a lot of time at the student center admiring pretty girls. This lasted until he got an unsigned note (undoubtedly from Wyatt) saying: "Congratulations on your work. When are you going to start?" Majors became a perpetual-motion machine thereafter, assuming every task he could find to help the program. Thus was launched one of the most successful coaching careers in college football history.

After paying his dues as an assistant on several staffs, Majors began itching to run his own program. That's when he got some cautionary advice from former Vol assistant John Barnhill: "You need to get your feet wet sooner or later. But you don't want to get in up to your ass in mud."

Johnny wondered whether he'd done just that shortly after taking the reins at Iowa State in 1968 at age thirty-two. He gradually rebuilt the long-downtrodden Cyclones into a respectable team, however, and was tabbed Big Eight Coach of the Year in 1971. He then assumed another losing program,

The Old "Limp Leg" Still Works

Johnny Majors was a master of the "limp leg" style of running—showing a defender a leg and then quickly withdrawing it and darting in the other direction. This served him well at Huntland High School, enabling him to lead the state of Tennessee in scoring in 1950 (161 points), 1951 (153), and 1952 (213).

Arriving at the University of Tennessee as the program's smallest freshman, however, the 144-pounder figured the tricks that worked at Huntland High might not work against the bigger, stronger, faster college boys. Unsure whether he possessed the talent to compete at the major college level, he fretted that he'd embarrass himself by proving to be the worst player on the team.

Fortunately these worries ended the day the Volunteers held their first scrimmage. Majors made a 7-yard run, then a 15-yarder. Following another nifty run, he was picking himself up from the turf when he heard a booming voice call out, "Who's that number 10?"

The voice belonged to the legendary General Robert R. Neyland, who had just become athletic director after a remarkable stint as Tennessee's head coach. Vol aide Farmer Johnson quickly responded, "General, that's Majors. From Huntland."

Johnson was understandably proud. After all, he had been the coach who signed the undersized tailback.

"I guess he was thrilled because he felt vindicated," Majors recalled. "As for me, I was thrilled because I wasn't dead."

Johnny made several more nice runs before the scrimmage ended and then rushed to a nearby drug store to call home.

"Daddy," he shouted into the phone, "they miss tackles up here, just like they do in high school!"

Pittsburgh, which he quickly turned into a national power. He was National Coach of the Year in '73 and again in '76, when he guided the Panthers to the national title.

While celebrating his greatest achievement, Majors faced his greatest decision. Tennessee had fallen on hard times, so the obvious choice to resurrect the struggling program was native son John Terrill Majors. Would he leave a national championship team at Pitt out of loyalty to his alma mater? The question haunted him for weeks.

"I wanted both jobs," Majors recalled years later, "but you couldn't do both. So I made the decision to go to Tennessee."

The rebuilding effort progressed slowly. His first eight years on the job produced a modest 51–39–3 record. His program finally turned the corner in 1985, posting three watershed victories that established Tennessee as a team on the rise.

The first occurred September 28 against top-ranked Auburn, led by Heisman Trophy favorite Bo Jackson. *Sports Illustrated* sent a writer and photographer to pay homage to Jackson's brilliance but wound up reversing its field and slanting the story toward rifle-armed Tennessee quarterback Tony Robinson, who guided the spunky Volunteers to a stunning 38–20 upset.

The second occurred October 19 against Alabama at Birmingham's Legion Field. Robinson suffered a season-ending knee injury in the fourth quarter, leaving the game with Tennessee clinging to a tenuous 16–14 lead. The Crimson Tide was methodically marching to the winning score when Vol linebacker Dale Jones leaped in front of Bama quarterback Mike Shula, deflected a pass as it left Shula's fingertips, and then made a juggling interception as he tumbled to the ground. Some witnesses hailed it as the single greatest defensive play in Volunteer history. If it wasn't, it was awfully close.

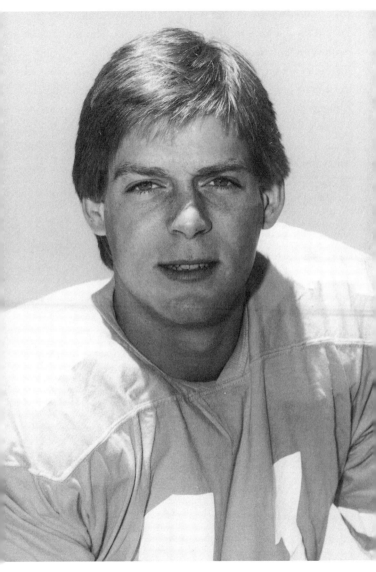

A modern-day Cinderella story, Daryl Dickey went from backup quarter-back to Sugar Bowl MVP during the course of the 1985 season.

Following the Bama game, Majors faced a decision that would set the tone for the rest of the season: Should he stick with number-two quarterback Daryl Dickey, who was shaky in his relief stint against the Tide, or should he go with talented freshman Jeff Francis? Majors opted for experience, and the strategy paid glorious dividends.

Dickey wound up leading the Vols to five wins and a tie in their final six games, plus the Southeastern Conference championship. He then outdueled Miami's Testaverde to earn recognition as MVP of the 1986 Sugar Bowl.

Suddenly Johnny Majors was the toast of Tennessee.

Again.

Peyton's Place

His reputation as a high school superstar and the son of a college football legend had preceded him, yet the scrawny teenager was just another freshman quarterback when he joined Tennessee's huddle in the second half of the 1994 Florida game. So, with the homestanding Volunteers on the wrong end of a 24–0 score, the first words out of his mouth were not warmly received by his veteran teammates.

"All right, guys," he said, "we're going to take it down the field and score."

Clearly annoyed by the pep talk, offensive tackle Jason Layman snarled, "Shut the bleep up and call the bleepin' play."

Welcome to college football, Peyton Manning.

"When you're getting beat 24–0 on your home field, you don't want to hear that from an eighteen-year-old," Layman explained. "But Peyton's confident. I like that."

Layman would like the young quarterback a lot better as the season progressed, and so would the Volunteer nation.

Assuming the first-team job two weeks later, after Tennessee had lost three of its first four games, Manning guided the Vols to a stunning 10–9 upset of number-seventeen Washington State. The following Saturday he led them to a 38–21 defeat of Arkansas. A potential game-winning touchdown pass to Joey Kent was broken up at the goal line in the final minute of a 17–13 loss to tenth-ranked Alabama, but Manning would not lose again. Gaining confidence each week, he polished off South Carolina, Memphis, Kentucky, and Vanderbilt and then

Peyton Manning became Tennessee's first-team quarterback in Game 5 of his freshman year and kept the job for the next three and one-half seasons.

dissected Virginia Tech 45–23 in the Gator Bowl. With a 7–1 record as a starting quarterback and three years of eligibility remaining, he appeared destined for greatness.

He was.

Following a workmanlike 27–7 defeat of East Carolina in the 1995 opener, Tennessee found itself unable to stop Georgia tailback Robert Edwards in Game 2. The showdown turned into a track meet but Manning met the challenge, completing twenty-six of thirty-eight passes for 349 yards and two touchdowns in a thrilling 30–27 victory.

"That was the first time I felt I took my game to another level," he said, "and that was the first truly big game we were able to win."

The college football world didn't realize it, but Manning and the Vols were on the verge of becoming an unstoppable offensive force. They scored thirty-seven points in a Game 3 loss at Florida and then tacked on fifty-two against Mississippi State, thirty-one against Oklahoma State, and forty-nine against Arkansas. Manning was red-hot in the latter, completing thirty-five of forty-six passes for 384 yards and four touchdowns.

Still, Tennessee was a slight underdog as it traveled to Birmingham to face seventh-ranked Alabama on October 14. That was understandable; the Vols hadn't beaten the Tide in nine years, and talk of a "Bama Jinx" was rampant.

Manning needed all of one play to quiet this talk, hitting Kent in perfect stride on a post pattern that turned into an 80-yard touchdown play. Manning threw two more touchdown passes before the night was through, finishing twenty of twenty-nine for 301 yards. He also scored untouched on a bootleg following a deviously convincing play fake, as the Volunteers romped 41–14.

"Arkansas was probably my best game," he recalled, "but Alabama was the most fun."

The fun continued as Manning blitzed South Carolina 56–21 to conclude the greatest month any Volunteer quarterback ever enjoyed. His cumulative stats for three October games showed seventy-one completions in ninety-five attempts (75.8 percent) for exactly 900 yards and eleven touchdowns. The Vols outscored Arkansas, Alabama, and South Carolina by a combined 146–66 during this incredible stretch.

Manning returned to Earth in November but still led the Big Orange past Southern Mississippi 42–0, Kentucky 34–31, and Vanderbilt 12–7. Coolly efficient in a rain-drenched Citrus Bowl game, he guided Tennessee to a 20–14 defeat of Ohio State, which had been ranked number one just a few weeks earlier. Coming off a season in which he led the Volunteers to an 11–1 record and a number-two national ranking, Manning had an 18–2 record as a starting quarterback and a growing legion of admirers. Even his dad, former Ole Miss All-American Archie Manning, was impressed.

"I knew Peyton's work ethic was good and that he was very anxious to learn when he got to Tennessee," Archie said. "What I didn't expect was for him to be this good this fast."

"You are looking at the top quarterback in the country," ESPN football analyst Mike Gottfried said in November 1995. "I don't think there's much doubt about that."

Pro Football Weekly's Joel Buchsbaum was even more lavish in his praise, noting: "In perfect honesty, there is nobody who can hold a candle to Tennessee's Peyton Manning. Manning is just a sophomore, but he probably deserves the Heisman, and if he were in the NFL Draft, he would be the first player picked."

Manning didn't opt for the NFL Draft, and he didn't win

the Heisman. He finished sixth. With two years of eligibility remaining, however, it seemed a cinch that there would be a Heisman in his future.

Entering his junior season, Manning was the poster boy for all that is good in college football. An A student in the class-room and a positive influence in the community, he seemed almost too good to be true. He was a class act, probably because he had grown up in a class family.

Peyton had passed for 7,207 yards and ninety-two touch-downs at New Orleans's Isidore Newman High School, earning recognition as the Gatorade National Player of the Year in 1993. Still, his most impressive accomplishment during this time came not in the face of a blitz but in the face of a family setback. Cooper Manning, forced to give up foot-ball due to a spinal condition discovered during his freshman year at Ole Miss, wrote a moving letter telling Peyton he would be playing for both of them from that point forward. Peyton was so touched that he switched his jersey from 14, his dad's high school number, to 18, Cooper's college number.

As his prep career drew to a close, Peyton faced pressures far beyond those encountered by most prospects. His father had been the most famous player in Ole Miss history. His mother, Olivia, had been a homecoming queen there. And, of course, Cooper was a sophomore at the school. Given the strength of these ties, Peyton informed his family on the eve of his college commitment that he would be attending Ole Miss. His dad's response was unexpected. Archie said he should make the decision that was best for himself, not his family. Peyton went public for Tennessee the next day.

Weeks later, Vol offensive coordinator David Cutcliffe visited the Manning home in New Orleans to familiarize Peyton and his famous father with the Tennessee offense. He

Peyton Manning attended Tennessee with the full support of his parents, loyal Ole Miss alumni Archie and Olivia Manning.

found only half of his audience attentive.

"Coach Cutcliffe was showing me the plays," Peyton recalled, "and we looked over and my dad was snoring. It was kinda revealing that he didn't care . . . that I was going to learn Coach Cutcliffe's style."

Archie conceded as much, noting, "Maybe in some indirect way I was saying, 'You're his coach. I'm his daddy. I don't want to know the ins and outs of the Tennessee offense.'"

Although he never wavered after picking Tennessee, Peyton had seriously considered the pass-happy Florida Gators.

"One thing I was looking for was my best opportunity to play in my second year," he said. "Florida had Danny Wuerffel and Eric Kresser coming back. Tennessee had nobody coming back."

The Vols had someone coming in, though—the talented Texan Branndon Stewart, who actually was rated ahead of Manning by some recruiting services. They would wage a heated battle for playing time as Volunteer freshmen in 1994. Manning eventually got the starting job and more playing time, but Stewart garnered considerable fan support thanks to a stronger arm and quicker feet. Even as the quarterback controversy raged, Manning handled himself with remarkable poise and grace—a testament to his father's influence.

"What Peyton has learned from his dad, and will continue to learn," Olivia Manning once noted, "is not really how to play football but how to be a football player."

Peyton Manning would prove to be the ultimate football player—respectful to his coaches, loyal to his teammates, accommodating to the press, and approachable to the fans.

"I think it's flattering," he once said of the attention from boosters and media. "One thing I've always believed is that if they're not asking for your autograph and not wanting to talk to you, then you're not playing very well . . . here in Tennessee, especially."

Manning's patience with people intent on shoving a tape recorder or an autograph pen in his face had been forged as he watched the twilight years of Archie's pro career. "Growing up in the environment I did, I saw the bad guys walk through the media, walk through little kids, and kind of push them to the side," he said. "Then I watched my dad, who always took time to do the interviews and the autographs. So I got a good experience there, and I've always taken time to do it . . . and kept a smile on my face."

How's This for an Encore?

Considering Peyton Manning's remarkable exploits as a quarterback at the University of Tennessee, some observers assumed his career in the National Football League couldn't possibly live up to the lofty standards of his college days.

Simply put, they were wrong. If anything, Manning has been even more dynamic as a professional than he was as a collegian. Since his selection by the Indianapolis Colts with the first pick in the 1998 NFL Draft, he has continued to pad his statistics and strengthen his legacy.

Colts head coach Tony Dungy noted following the 2003 season that Manning had "a phenomenal year," and that's no exaggeration. Manning posted a career-best 67 percent completion rate. He threw 29 touchdown passes and a career-low 10 interceptions. His 4,267 passing yards—the second-best total of his career—marked the fifth consecutive season he has cracked the 4,000-yard level, a feat unprecedented in NFL history. And he earned a bid to the Pro Bowl for the fourth season in a row.

Already recognized by his fans and his peers as one of the game's all-time greats, Manning signed a contract on March 2, 2004 that indicates he also has the respect of his bosses. The deal calls for $98 million spread over seven years—not counting incentives—and includes a mind-boggling $34.5 million signing bonus.

In typical low-key fashion, Manning shrugged off questions about the big payoff by noting: "I don't even like to use the word 'money.'"

With a bank balance *that* spectacular, words are inadequate anyhow.

Though best known for his spectacular passing, Manning often froze opposing defenders with his deft ball-handling skills.

Manning had plenty of reason to smile during his Tennessee career. He was virtually unstoppable and the Vols were virtually unbeatable—except when they played Florida. After trouncing Nevada–Las Vegas 62–3 and UCLA 35–20 to open the 1996 season, the Big Orange self-destructed in a 35–29 Game 3 loss to the Gators. Tennessee outgained Florida by nearly 200 yards (501 to 304) as Manning compiled thirty-seven completions in sixty-five attempts for 492 yards—all school records. He lost four interceptions and a fumble, however, that led to fourteen Florida points.

"Dad said he was proud of me," Peyton said afterward. "He and I have talked about this for a long time—the fact that there was going to be a game in my career like this. You have games where you're throwing interceptions left and right. I just picked a bad game to do it."

Then, noting that Archie had thrown six interceptions in a 1968 loss to Tennessee, Peyton flashed a sheepish grin and said, "At least I didn't throw that many."

Following an open date, Tennessee would travel to Memphis to face Ole Miss, whose fans revered Archie as a legend and reviled Peyton as a traitor. Both Mannings were uncomfortable with the media blitz that preceded the game.

"I don't always look at him as a football player; I look at him as my little boy," Archie said. "This puts a lot of pressure on a kid—dealing with a tough loss to Florida, then all of this hoopla about playing against Ole Miss."

By the eve of the big game, however, Peyton had regained his composure and refocused his energies. Recognizing this as the two chatted by telephone, Archie turned to Olivia and remarked, "Ole Miss is in for a tough night, because he's ready."

Peyton was ready, all right. With his parents watching from the stands, he completed eighteen of twenty-two passes for 242 yards, as the Vols romped 41–3. Awarded a game ball, he handed it off to his dad with the comment, "This one is special."

Archie showed that he, too, is special. Hounded by the media after the game, he admitted that the matchup put him in a "funny situation" but insisted his loyalties were never divided.

"People kept asking me a kind of ridiculous question: Who are you for?" he said. "I'm for my son. I pull for *him*. My family's always been paramount with me. But I'll tell you this: I didn't pull against Ole Miss."

Tennessee would finish 10–2 by winning seven of its eight remaining games, including lopsided defeats of Arkansas (55–14), Kentucky (56–10), and Northwestern in the Citrus Bowl (48–28). In an amazing coincidence, Manning had thrown exactly the same number of passes in 1996 he had a year earlier (380) with one fewer completion (243, down from 244). His 3,287 passing yards eclipsed the school record of 2,969 he had set the year before.

With most of the key players due to return from a 1996 team that finished number nine nationally, the Volunteers appeared poised to make a serious run at the national championship in 1997. The only question was: Would Manning be back to lead the charge?

He wrestled with the decision for months and then called a news conference to announce his verdict just two weeks before the start of spring practice. After sitting stone-faced while waiting to be introduced, he built the suspense for several nerve-racking minutes before finally getting to the point: "I've made up my mind, and I don't expect to ever look back . . . I'm going to stay at the University of Tennessee."

The crowd paused briefly while absorbing these words, then erupted into a roar so overwhelming that the conference could not resume for a full thirty-five seconds. Eventually Manning explained that he "just wanted to come back, be a college student one more year, and enjoy the entire experience." He then made three points abundantly clear:

— He was not coming back to beat Florida.
— He was not coming back to win the national title.
— He was not coming back to win the Heisman Trophy.

Those words would prove prophetic; he would not accomplish any of the three.

After opening his senior season with 52–17 and 30–24 wins over Texas Tech and UCLA, respectively, Manning saw his record against Florida drop to 0–3 with a 33–20 loss at Gainesville. He completed twenty-nine of fifty-one passes for 353 yards and three touchdowns but threw an interception that Tony George returned eighty-nine yards for a touchdown to give the top-ranked Gators an early lead they never surrendered.

Bouncing back to win the next six games in a row, Manning and the Vols carried an 8–1 record into their November 22 showdown at Kentucky, led by star quarterback Tim Couch. Dubbed "the Shootout at UK Corral," the eagerly anticipated duel would prove to be an unforgettable air show. Couch completed thirty-five of fifty passes for 476 yards and two touchdowns. Manning was even better, completing twenty-five of thirty-five throws for 523 yards and five touchdowns as Tennessee prevailed 59–31. The two potent passers combined for 999 yards, and the two offenses piled up an amazing 1,329 total yards.

"I've been in games that were built up to be like this," Manning said afterward, "but this is the first one that turned out to be this way. You score a touchdown, then you're right back on the sidelines saying, 'We've got to score again, guys.'"

Peyton's Place Becomes U-Tee

With 4:24 remaining in the 1998 Orange Bowl Game, Tennessee's starting quarterback stood quietly on the sidelines, having passed for a mere 134 yards to that point. With Nebraska leading 42–9 and Peyton Manning nursing a bad knee, Vol coaches decided that the only thing he'd pass in the closing minutes was the torch. After four years as Tennessee's starting quarterback, Manning symbolically handed the job to backup Tamaurice "Tee" Martin.

Would there be life after Manning? Yes. Martin completed four of four passes for 53 yards, capping an 80-yard march with a 3-yard touchdown throw to Andy McCullough and then tossing a two-point conversion pass to Travis Stephens.

Peyton's Place had become U–Tee.

Despite Martin's impressive performance on that closing drive against Nebraska, many Vol fans figured Tennessee would suffer from PMS (Post-Manning Syndrome) in the fall of '98. They were wrong. Martin rallied from a sluggish start to guide Tennessee to a 13–0 record and the program's first national title in forty-seven years.

The torch had been passed.

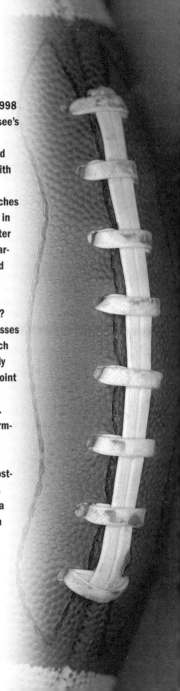

The Kentucky game would prove to be the high point of Manning's senior season, which went downhill rapidly from that point. He struggled in a season-ending 17–10 defeat of Vanderbilt and then had to rally the mistake-prone Vols for a 30–29 defeat of Auburn in the Southeastern Conference Championship Game. After losing the Heisman Trophy to Michigan cornerback Charles Woodson—the first defensive player ever to win the honor—Manning would play his final college game on a severely injured knee. Limping noticeably, he completed twenty-one of thirty-one passes for a mere 134 yards as the Vols lost to Nebraska 42–17 in the Orange Bowl. It was a humiliating end to a heroic college career. Manning finished his college days as the SEC's career record-holder in completions (863), passing yards (11,201), completion percentage (62.5), and lowest interception percentage (2.39). His yardage total was the third-highest in college football history.

The football world had not heard the last of Peyton Manning, however. Heisman voters declined to tab him the country's premier football player, yet he won the Sullivan Award as the country's premier amateur athlete. Tennessee renamed a campus street in his honor. Tabbed with the first pick in the 1998 National Football League Draft, Manning has come to be recognized as the game's premier passer. A perennial all-pro, he appears destined for the Hall of Fame . . . which just shows how much a guy can accomplish once he learns to "shut the bleep up and call the bleepin' play."

The Road to the 1998 National Title

D own 33–31 with 1:48 to play and a fourth-and-7 at its own 35 yard line to overcome, the 1998 Tennessee Vols were one play from losing the first game of their post–Peyton Manning era. Tamaurice "Tee" Martin, faced with the awesome responsibility of following Manning, took a deep breath and tried to calm his nerves as he scanned the Syracuse defense and began barking his signals.

Taking the snap from center, he nimbly dropped back to pass and looked hurriedly to his left. Spotting sophomore Cedrick Wilson temporarily in the open, Martin cocked his powerful right arm and let fly. As the ball hurtled toward Wilson, Syracuse cornerback Will Allen did likewise. Approaching from opposite directions, ball and defender arrived almost simultaneously—Allen hitting Wilson in the back maybe $\frac{1}{10}$ of a second before the ball hit Wilson in the shoulder pads and then ricocheted to the turf.

What happened during the next few seconds was almost surrealistic, resembling one of those super slow-mo scenes popular in action movies. Martin, convinced there was inter-ference on the play, looked to the officials for confirmation.

"I was pulling my jersey like I had a flag on my hip, trying to get somebody's attention," he said.

Tee Martin exhibited a powerful arm and quick feet in guiding Tennessee to a national title in 1998, his first year as the Vols' starting quarterback.

Wilson, the intended receiver, leaped to his feet and protested that he had been hit before the ball arrived. "I was very worried about not seeing a flag," he said, "and that's when I got up and questioned the refs."

His heart sank when a member of the Southeastern Conference officiating crew waved his arms to signal the pass "incomplete," but Wilson's spirits lifted a second later when a late penalty flag sailed into the area. Back judge Lee Dyer had been so far from the play that he couldn't hurl his flag all the way to the spot in one heave; he had to pick it up and toss it a second time.

"The guy in the back finally threw the flag," Wilson noted. "The guy right by me didn't."

A 15-yard penalty was assessed, sustaining the drive and giving the Big Orange a first-and-10 at midfield. No one knew it at the time, but the Tennessee Volunteers had just taken their first step on the road to a national championship.

Three runs by Jamal Lewis and a 17-yard pass from Martin to Peerless Price moved the ball to the Syracuse 10 yard line, then Jeff Hall kicked a 27-yard field goal as time expired to give Tennessee a dramatic 34–33 victory.

Syracuse quarterback Donovan McNabb had been heroic in defeat—twenty-two completions in twenty-eight attempts for 300 yards and two touchdowns—but Tennessee had some heroes, too. Lewis finished with 143 yards on twenty carries. Martin completed just nine of twenty-six pass attempts for 143 yards but set up a touchdown with a 55-yard run and showed remarkable poise on the game-winning drive. Price caught six passes for 87 yards and two touchdowns. Hall nailed two field-goal tries, including the clutch game-winner.

Still, the biggest play of the game was made by a guy wearing a striped shirt, not an orange one. Had Dyer not made

Receiver Peerless Price contributed numerous big plays in '98, including this 100-yard kickoff return against Alabama.

the interference call, Tennessee would have started the '98 season 0–1.

"Thank God the ref called it," Price said.

Even Tennessee's most rabid fans were not surprised by the Game 1 struggle. After all, the Big Orange had lost superstars Manning, Leonard Little, Marcus Nash, and Terry Fair to the previous spring's NFL Draft. Noting the mass exodus of blue-chip talent, preseason prognosticators pegged the '98 Vols for mediocrity. These insults merely served to put a chip on the shoulder of Tennessee's players. The more vocal their critics became, the more tightly knit the Vols became.

Given the close call against Syracuse, Tennessee seemed a real longshot to win Game 2 against Florida, which had beaten the Big Orange five times in a row by an average margin of nearly seventeen points. This team had a date with destiny, however. That became evident when Florida blew one touchdown by fumbling at the goal line, blew another touchdown when John Capel stepped out of bounds on what would have been a 100-yard kickoff return, and then blew the game when its kicker hooked a chip-shot field goal in overtime. Martin completed just seven of twenty passes for 63 yards but made a crucial third-down scramble to set up another game-winning field goal by Hall, as the Volunteers prevailed 20–17 in overtime. Tennessee's average victory margin in the first two games was a scant two points, but the Big Orange was 2–0, and that's all that mattered.

After completing fourteen of nineteen pass attempts for 234 yards and four touchdowns in a 42–7 blowout of lowly Houston, Martin assumed that Tennessee's coaches would loosen the reins a bit. They didn't. He threw just fourteen passes, completing five, in a 17–9 Game 4 victory at Auburn. A frustrated Martin would later recall, "It was like I was being contained by my own coach, like I was in my own jail. When they finally let me out, I was like a little kid in a candy store."

The coaches "let him out" only because Lewis had suffered a season-ending knee injury at Auburn, leaving the Big Orange without the centerpiece of its offense. Retooling the attack around their second-best offensive weapon, Vol coaches finally put the offense in Martin's hands. He responded by throwing two first-half interceptions in Game 6 against Georgia and then atoning with two third-quarter touchdown passes that fueled a 22–3 victory.

It Was Teamwork More than Talent

I t isn't always about talent. The University of Tennessee football program produced some of the finest players in college football during the 1990s, including two quarterbacks who were Heisman Trophy runners-up—Heath Shuler and Peyton Manning.

The '90s cast also included such future National Football League players as offensive linemen Charles McRae, Antone Davis, Jason Layman, Bubba Miller, Jeff Smith, Trey Teague, Tom Myslinski, and Bernard Dafney; running backs James Stewart, Charlie Garner, Jay Graham, and Jamal Lewis; receivers Carl Pickens, Alvin Harper, and Marcus Nash; defensive linemen Chuck Smith, Chris Mims, Shane Burton, Leonard Little, Todd Kelly, Shane Bonham, Steve White, and Ben Talley; linebackers Darryl Hardy and Scott Galyon; and defensive backs Dale Carter, Jeremy Lincoln, DeRon Jenkins, J. J. McCleskey, and Terry Fair.

Yet none of these players was in the lineup when the 1998 Vols beat Florida State 23–16 to win the program's first national title in forty-seven years. The '98 team was basically a no-name bunch.

"I've been here nine years, and this is the fourth-most talented team we've had, but it's the best team," tight ends coach Mark Bradley said following the title game. "There's a difference. We had chemistry."

That chemistry was built on a foundation of unselfishness and teamwork.

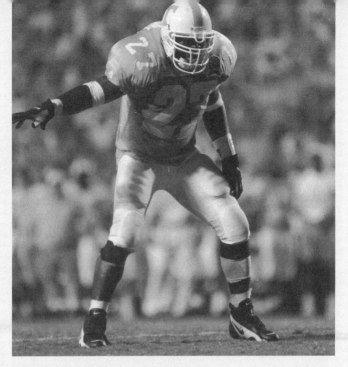

Fiery linebacker Al Wilson was the emotional leader of the '98 national champs, willing the overachieving team to victory at times.

"Not one of them cares who gets the credit," strength coach John Stucky said. "That's what's so special."

Cornerback Steve Johnson said, "It's like a close-knit family. We had no superstars. We lost all the superstars last year to the NFL."

Despite this lack of marquee names, the '98 Volunteers played with tremendous confidence, individually and collectively.

"I've never been around a team so confident, so relaxed, or one that had so much fun playing football," linebacker Al Wilson said. "The attitude we took into each game—to be the best team on the field—is what really set us apart from all other teams."

He must have been correct. Most of the key players returned for the 1999 season, but the attitude was different. As a result, a 1999 Tennessee team picked to repeat as national champions finished 9–3.

It isn't always about talent.

His confidence bolstered, Martin would never be the same again. After guiding Tennessee past Alabama 35–18, he broke an NCAA record by completing his first twenty-three passes at South Carolina, finishing twenty-three of twenty-four for 315 yards and four touchdowns as the Vols romped 49–14. At game's end, teammates dumped a barrel of iced Gatorade on his head—finally cooling off the hottest passer in college football history. When asked afterward if he'd give himself an A for the performance, Martin humbly replied, "Yeah, I got an A today. I missed three checks, though, so I guess it was an A-minus."

Following a routine dismantling of Alabama-Birmingham in Game 9, Tennessee moved to number one in the national polls. Alas, having gained respect, the Vols lost the chip on their shoulders . . . and nearly lost Game 10, as well. The Arkansas Razorbacks, with possession of the ball near midfield and a 24–22 lead, needed only to survive the remaining 1:47 to seal the monumental upset. They couldn't, thanks to one of the freakiest plays in the game's history. Quarterback Clint Stoerner tripped as he backed away from center, losing his grip on the football as he tried vainly to break his fall. The ball squirted a few yards backward, and Tennessee defensive tackle Billy Ratliffe pounced on it at the Arkansas 43 yard line. Five plays later, with just twenty-eight seconds left on the clock, Travis Henry dived into the end zone to give the Vols a heart-stopping 28–24 triumph.

"The Good Lord," Tennessee head man Phillip Fulmer said, "may have been shining on us tonight."

The Volunteers subsequently pounded Kentucky (59–21) and Vanderbilt (41–0) to clinch the Southeastern Conference Eastern Division title and move to 11–0. Still, they were no lock to play in the Fiesta Bowl for the national title. Second-ranked Kansas State (11–0) and third-ranked UCLA (10–0) also were unbeaten heading into the final weekend of regular-season play. Fate again smiled on Tennessee, however, as Miami shocked UCLA 49–45 and Texas A&M knocked off Kansas State 36–33 in double overtime. Tennessee needed only to beat West Division champ Mississippi State in the SEC Championship Game later that evening to guarantee a Fiesta Bowl bid. Like UCLA and Kansas State, however, the Vols found December 5 to be a difficult day for favorites. When Mississippi State's Kevin Prentiss returned a punt 83 yards to give the Bulldogs a 14–10 lead with just 8:43 remaining, "Upset Saturday" appeared ready to claim its third victim. So why was Vol linebacker Al Wilson laughing?

"I knew what it was about to be like," he said. "I knew our guys were going to step up, man. We'd been there before, and you could see it in their eyes."

He was right. Martin moved the Vols to MSU's 41 yard line and then lofted a touchdown pass to Price that put Tennessee up 17–14 with 6:15 remaining. When the Vols recovered a fumble on the first play of Mississippi State's ensuing possession, Martin threw his second touchdown pass in twenty-eight seconds—this one covering 26 yards to Cedrick Wilson. Minutes after the mind-numbing 24–14 victory concluded, Tennessee agreed to meet Florida State in the Fiesta Bowl, with the national title at stake.

Shortly thereafter, oddsmakers did the Big Orange a huge favor. By establishing second-ranked FSU as a four-point favorite over top-ranked Tennessee, they restored the chip to the Volunteers' shoulders that had been missing since the Arkansas game. The final piece of the puzzle was in place; the inner fire had been rekindled.

"I don't think we're mentioned in the same breath with the Florida States and Nebraskas and Floridas," Price grumbled.

"We have to win a national championship if we want to even be considered in the same breath."

As they had done throughout August and September, Tennessee's players drew incentive from insult. They broke from each huddle during Fiesta Bowl preparations with the chant "One, two, three . . . underdogs!" By kickoff, the Volunteers were more than a great football team; they were a pack of snarling pit bulls straining at the leash.

Price was at least part greyhound, though. Late in the first quarter he sliced through the Florida State secondary for a 76-yard reception that carried to the 12 yard line. Moments later, a 4-yard swing pass to fullback Shawn Bryson gave Tennessee a 7–0 lead. Cornerback Dwayne Goodrich showed some greyhound lineage, too, returning a second-quarter interception 54 yards for a score that padded the lead to 14–0.

Nothing came easily for the '98 Volunteers, however, and the national title would be no exception. Their lead cut to 14–9, they faced a third-and-9 at their 21 yard line with nine and one-half minutes remaining. Rather than run something safe and trust the defense to protect its tenuous lead, Tennessee gambled by calling "69 All Go," a play in which all three wide receivers run fly patterns. Price sailed past Florida State cornerback Mario Edwards, made an over-the-shoulder catch of Martin's perfectly thrown bomb near the Seminole 30 yard line, and then sprinted into the end zone, widening the gap to 20–9. The breathtaking play sealed Tennessee's first national title since 1951, although late scores by each team moved the final score to 23–16.

Stung by pregame hoopla pinpointing FSU's Peter Warrick as the title game's key player, Price the Peerless clearly had outclassed Peter the Great. Whereas Warrick was limited to one catch for 7 yards, Price parlayed his four catches into

*Peerless Price churns toward the end zone after making the catch that
clinched Tennessee's title-winning defeat of Florida State.*

An elated Phillip Fulmer proudly displays the Sears Trophy after capturing the Big Orange's first national title in forty-seven years.

199 yards and Most Valuable Player recognition. All but forgotten in the postgame celebration was the fact that Price nearly didn't make it to Tempe. Following Tennessee's humiliating 42–17 Orange Bowl loss to Nebraska the previous January, he had been ready to turn pro rather than return for his senior year of college.

"I was leaning more toward leaving," he said. "I was down about losing, and I felt like this chapter of my life was over."

Fate intervened, however. Vinder Price, Peerless's mom, convinced him to return for his senior year by reminding him that he would be the team's go-to receiver. Twelve months later she was . . . well, Vinder-cated. Meanwhile, her son and his teammates were celebrated.

The Volunteers had kept their date with destiny. Now they could look back on a march to the national title that began with a pass Cedrick Wilson didn't catch and ended with a pass Peerless Price did.

About the Author

Randy Moore is editor of *Rocky Top News*, a specialty publication devoted to University of Tennessee sports.

He began following the University of Tennessee football program as a teenaged fan in the early 1960s. After graduating from East Tennessee State University, Randy took a sports reporting position with the *Knoxville Journal* in 1974, working his way onto the Vol football beat in 1984. He served as the primary beat reporter from 1986 to 1991, helping the *Journal* to achieve recognition as the top-ranked sports section nationally in its circulation class.

Randy has covered roughly 300 Tennessee football games, as well as Vol and Lady Vol basketball, a Little League World Series, Atlanta Braves baseball, and two world heavyweight championship boxing cards. He lives in Mosheim, some 60 miles north of Knoxville.